Just a Thought

RULES FOR CIVIL LIVING

A THRIVING GUIDE.
DON'T JUST SURVIVE.
CHOOSE TO THRIVE!

SAMUEL BRIAN HILL

ISBN 978-1-64003-022-0 (Paperback)
ISBN 978-1-64003-023-7 (Digital)

Covenant Books, Inc.
11661 Hwy 707
Murrells Inlet, SC 29576
www.covenantbooks.com

Contents

To my Eleanor and Josiah

I wrote these principles to live by to serve as a reference guide for your journey. Though I already know that you are both intelligent and studious, *Wisdom* grows with age and guidance. Although my desire is that the Bible be your ultimate resource guide for life, I hope that this collection of my principles, which I have learned from wiser people along my journey, will serve you well also. I charge you to live a life worthy of the cost that has been paid for you.

Being your father has been the greatest honor of my life, and I thank God daily for entrusting you to me and your Mom. You are the two greatest blessings of my life, and I love you to the moon times infinity. Choose to *Live* your life for the *Glory* of God, the *Growth* of His *Kingdom*, and the *Benefit* of the people.

To the Young Generation

I wrote this because I believe there is more to you than society expects of you. These principles will not make you a success. They will not miraculously cause you to be rich. They will not inherently produce good or truth or value in your life. In fact, merely reading these rules will do nothing for you. However, if you choose to apply these principles, you will so position yourself to live a successful life, to build wealth, and to be an individual of integrity who speaks truth with character. If you choose to apply these values to your life, *You* will live a life of *Value*. Be *Bold*. Break *Trends*. Seek *Wisdom*. Don't just survive. Choose to *Thrive*!

In Gratitude

This is the part where I am going to share my deepest gratitude to some of those individuals who are responsible for my journey. Most of these individuals are not "famous" by modern standards, but without them, you and I would not be sharing this collection of thoughts. Therefore, they are a *big deal*, and I must share a few thoughts about them. So here we go . . .

My wife, *Melissa*, is truly the most extraordinary woman I have ever encountered, and I find myself more grateful each day for her love and support. She is my *Partner in Life*, in parenting, in business and is my best friend. To be frank, had she not been brought into my life, I question where I would even be today. She is my *Sunshine*, my *Balance*, and my *Inspiration* to be a better man. Young men, I highly recommend you find your "Melissa" because it is impossible for you to achieve all your dreams without her. Young women, I highly recommend you live your life in such a way as to be like her, because if you do, you will make a lasting and eternal difference. *To my Melis, I Love you to the Moon and back! Thank you for choosing me, for not getting out of the car, for always supporting my dreams (regardless of how crazy they might be), and for being My Gal! I Love You, Slim!*

My Mom, *Myra J. Thornton Hill*, without her, I am not sure this book of thoughts would have ever reached completion in time for publication! Over the last five days, she literally went through every chapter with me, helped cut what was not necessary for this book, and even shared in this writing experience by expressing her thoughts. Out of this experience, I was reminded how much she and I share in thinking, purpose, and determination—from which

I am quite convinced she could have equally written this collection of thoughts with many of the same words and phrases! So please, young generation, never take for granted the *Value* of your *Mother*. Although you might conflict on some or *many* issues, you just might find in the distance it is due to a similar reflection in the mirror of personality For those of you who do not have such an amazing woman in your life because of her poor choices or the losses of life, I pray that your Creator brings such a woman into your life for your journey to fill the gaps, such as my Mom has been for me and even continues to do now in my adult years.

To you, Mom, *Thank You*! You have always been my "Biggest Fan" and for that I am *Eternally Grateful*! You built in me the courage and *Faith* to believe for something more . . . to hold in life for the humanly impossible. I am so appreciative of all your sacrifice so my dreams could thrive. I stand here today only because it is your shoulders which have held me up. Love you, Mom!

—Your little man

My Dad, *Sam W. Hill*, who taught me what being a *Man* really meant. He worked extremely hard to give us a better life. He was steady and dependable, by which we moved out of extreme poverty into a better life. He showed me what a *Solid Work Ethic* really looks like . . . and I have strived to follow his example daily. He taught me how to catch a fish, shoot a gun, change a tire, drive a car, tie down a load of 6" x 20' pipe and a multitude of "Manly" things! I worked with him at the lumberyard as a preteen every summer and then at the plumbing and electrical warehouse until I left for college. When I lost my first tooth, he was there. When I played sports, he was *Always* there. When I worked hard, he was always there. When I was in my first wreck, *he* was there. When I walked across that stage as the first member of the Hill family to graduate college, *he* was there. And when, at the age of twenty-six, I opened my first company, *he* was there. You see my Dad taught me how to be a *Great Dad* to my kids with one simply lesson, repeated consistently over many years . . . He was there. And that taught me more than words

8

could ever express. My prayer for any of you reading this, who do not have such a man in your life, that you will find such a hero that cares about you for who you are, whom you can look up to for inspiration and guidance and whom you can trust to provide a steady word of direction through the struggles you will undoubtedly face. May your Creator send such a person into your life. For those of you who have a great dad, put this book down right now and go give him a hug (or at least send him a text if he's far away)! He will definitely appreciate it!

To you, Dad, *Thank You* for all your sacrifices and for always believing in me, even when I gave you many reasons not to, but most of all, *Thank You* for ALWAYS being there! Love ya, Dad!

—Your pal

* * *

My Appreciation List

(Because these people really made a difference in my life)

Moms and Dads Rodriguez (my In-Laws). Thank you for raising your Melissa in such a way that she is so *Amazing*, thank you for making me part of your family, and most of all, *Thank You* for entrusting Melissa to be my wife! I cannot say enough to express my Gratitude!

Aunt Margaret, thank you for telling me to *go* to *college* before I knew what a college was. Without your inspiration, I do not know how different my path would have been.

Grandaddy and Memaw Thornton, thank you for teaching me who Jesus was through your preaching, prayers, conversations, and mostly by your daily examples. I am *Eternally Grateful*.

Pop and Memaw Hill, thank you for making me the *apple* of your *eyes*! I learned strength through your journey.

Bro David, as my youth pastor, you put a microphone in my hand at the age of eleven and you believed I had something worthy to share. Thank you for walking through those very difficult teenage years guiding me. Your *eternal* impact on my life is without measure!

KT, thanks for believing in me when few did. Thank you also for not accepting my resignation as Youth Pastor . . . all five times! Much of my reach came from you holding up my arms. Thanks, bro!

LIFE 101, thank you to each of you *Amazing* "kids" for believing in the thoughts of a twenty-something guy on 10th Street! You are HUGE part of this book!

The CAVE, thank you to the mighty mass who expanded my view of what was possible. I remain grateful for each of you and the team with whom we served.

RADIUS, my *Gratitude* for you is immense. You folks were part of our lives as a light in a dark season. When our living room was an Adullam cave, you walked through that chapter and gave us reason to believe for more after our great loss. Thank you for your *Trust* and *Love*.

YFC OKC. To the YFC WEST Team, the YFC Staff, Board, Steering Crew of WEST and partners, thank you, for your support for almost a decade in reaching the students of West OKC with the Gospel through relationship on their school campuses. This book is a direct response to the need I have witnessed in an innumerable group of parentless boys and girls of this Young Generation. Thank you for your partnership in this worthy work of making an eternal impact!

Wes, thank you for agreeing to be on my "Board in Life." You are a true *Mentor, Friend*, and an inspiration to us all.

Howry, thank you for expanding my *Exposure*! Thank you for walking with me through the *War* and helping me see something beyond myself. You are a *True Friend*. Thanks for teaching me to always *Keep it about the Ketchup!*

Glenn, thank you for walking through this journey of making an impact on this Young Generation. You are my partner in this cause and you continue to inspire me with your drive. You are *my brother from another mother*, and I am so very grateful for your friendship!

K Fouts, thank you. Thank you for loving my family. Thank you for being there for us through the ups and downs of the year leading up to this book being published. If you had not believed in us and pushed us forward with your friendship and encouragement, I just do not know if this work would have reached completion. Thanks for being authentic and challenging me to believe for more. Even planes are possible . . . Thanks!

CR, thank you for believing in my dreams, bro, as much as you believe in yours! Thank you for making this book possible to all who it will reach. You are more than a friend; you are a brother in this cause!

To the *Masses* of *Teachers, Friends, Employees, "Kids,"* and *Partners* in this cause who have shared on my journey, *Thank You!* my heart overflows with gratitude for the amazing people God has placed along my path who walked beside me.

Introduction

Just a thought . . . *Few things are more powerful than a thought.* Everything that was ever created or destroyed began with the conception of a thought. Every villain with a dastardly plan and every hero who accepted the challenge all came to the stage of history by a mere thought. Every partnership, business, invention, innovation, discovery, and scientific breakthrough all began with a thought. The following principles and rules that I believe will serve you as a guide to thrive in your life, each began as a thought, which was sparked by an experience. I hold it to be true that all you truly own in this life is your response, and therefore this book is my collective response to those experiences and the thoughts they produced.

It is my hope and my prayer that this simple, yet hopefully provocative, gathering of my thoughts will *inspire you to live a successful life of expanding your own thoughts.* This book can accomplish nothing greater than sparking a thought in your mind and a pure purpose in your heart to accomplish something great, for it is after all merely a collection of my thoughts, which many are simply a response to someone else's thoughts . . . but let us not forget, as we begin, there are few things more powerful than a thought. Just a thought . . .

Founding Thought: *YOU MATTER*

YOU Matter. Your hopes. Your dreams. Your silent ambitions and wishes for the future all matter. And even though life and people may have said or made you think otherwise, you matter.

13

And before we begin, we must establish this key principle that which all the following principles will be founded upon, for if you do not believe that *You Matter*, nothing that follows will matter. You see, *Just as You Are*, you were made for a significant *Eternal* purpose. Your place on this Earth at this time is of *greater* significance than you can possibly imagine. According to the wise sage of old, Jeremiah (29:11), even before you were conceived, even beyond the creation of heaven and earth, *you* were a thought in the mind of the Divine Creator. And although people along your path may have caused you hurt, damage, and scars, he cares and has an ultimate plan: to redeem even your broken past and restore you too and magnificent future. And this is the fundamental thought that you need to begin at least to understand and grasp in order for any other thoughts in this following collection to be of any significance for your journey. *You Matter*.

So just in case, by some unfortunate situation, that no one has ever made you feel valuable or to be the treasurer that you were designed to be, let me express to you with the voice of all the ages, with the hope that is found in the *eternal*, you truly—as you are *You Matter*!

And this, my reader, is more than just a thought . . . This is an eternal principle . . . *You Matter!*

Now let's begin.

Rules for Civil Living

1

DO UNTO OTHERS AS YOU WOULD HAVE THEM DO UNTO YOU.

Seems simple, right? Then why do most people not live this way? We unfortunately live in a "every man for himself" world that focuses more on "What can I get from you?" rather than "What can I do for you?" Typically, operating with a servant's heart is viewed as a weakness, while destroying others to obtain the prize is viewed as a sign of strength. We have been taught "it's a dog-eat-dog world," so "win at all cost" and "let slip the dogs of war" on any that oppose us. Although this makes for great cinema and talk show drama, living with such a philosophy eventually leads to destruction. It is not a long-term plan for success . . . ever. Even if you accomplish your goal today, it will haunt you later along your journey. Although the bully covers his low self-esteem today by picking on the weak, he will pay the price as an employee, an athlete, a boss, or as a dad in years to come. Although the arrogant supervisor treats his employees with cruelty now, his actions will inevitably catch up to in the eyes of his supervisors or clients. *Evil will Never produce Good*. Even if it looks like a quick solution now, it will always end in destruction.

Every school has "it." That thing . . . you might not exactly know what it is, but you know you do *Not* want to *be* called *It*. In elementary schools, for years it was "Kooties," "Germs," or "Gay." When I was in first through fifth grade, at my school it was "Betty Germs." Betty was a girl who was the poorest of the poor in my school, and she did not always look or smell the nicest, which made her an easy target. What none of us knew at the time—and truth be told, probably did not care—was that Betty and her mom had nothing. Her mom worked hard to provide for her and her brother with little help. Although I would like to say that all of this changed as we grew out of "it," but unfortunately, "it" continued even into our high school years.

The second thing you know as a kid is you do not want to be *Connected* with the person who is "it." I will never forget the day, while we were walking through the halls of our high school, one of the other guys began a mindless chant about Betty and I being a thing. To my horror, a few of the other guys joined in with jokes and laughs. Realizing in that moment that my entire Junior and Senior years were on the line, I reacted. I did not consider the effects. I did not think about the power of my words. I certainly did not process that in the moment I would act in such a way that I would carry shame even into my adult life. In that moment, it was "dog-eat-dog," and I did what I thought was necessary to "survive." In the moment, I choose to join in with the crowd and be the bully rather than risk being *Connected* with the "it" that we as a people had connected to "Betty" . . . and I still regret it.

I should have defended Betty. I simply should have told the guys to knock it off and leave her alone. I could have even absorbed the jokes on myself. It really would not have been a major deal for me if I'm honest. I could have stopped the picking at that moment, but out of fear, I crumbled and became part of the problem.

I cannot tell you today the theme of the prom. I cannot tell you who we played in the homecoming game and even if we won. I cannot tell you the last name (and some first names) of every girl I went out with on my senior year. But I can vividly describe every part of the moment I sacrificed the feelings of someone else for the sake of my own comfort . . . and I regret it. Since that time, I found Betty on social media and wrote her an apology for my teenage cowardliness. She was beyond gracious, much more so than I deserved.

I consider it now, but had the roles been reversed and had I been in Betty's shoes, would I have been as kind as she or would I have taken the opportunity to hurt someone verbally who had hurt me with their unkind words? You see, if we live such a life by which we treat people with the same actions that we want to be treated, I am convinced our schools, neighborhoods, city, and *world* would be a much different place. And it is not complicated. We merely need to *think* before we speak and treat others with kindness, not cruelty. Will you make such a decision with me? Will you choose to do unto others as you would have them do unto you? If you do, I promise you will live a life with greater peace, joy, and hope. Just try it.

#2

JUST BECAUSE YOU CAN DOESN'T MEAN YOU SHOULD.

We live in a time of no-money down, rent to own, preapproved credit cards, and unsecured loans, which make it relatively easy to get deep in debt without a means or plan to repay it. With compound interest, a person can dig a financial pit before they can afford to buy their own shovel. Don't fall for the debt trap.

This principle applies to many other areas of our lives also. Too often we associate *Ability* with *Right* or *Approval*. The reality however is that MANY opportunities will present themselves that you *should not* pursue. Relationships. Offers. Jobs. Ideas. Proposals. Expansions. Moves. Even dreams and goals. Just because you can accept them or it does not mean they are the best opportunities or even the right one(s) for you.

I once bought a car because I could. It was a BMW 5 series, black on black with custom rims and the sport suspension package. It was gorgeous, mean, clean, nice, cool, sweet, wicked, and a few other words that go all the way back to 1985. It was supposed to be a status symbol. It was to be a sign that as an entrepreneur, I had arrived. I had driven onto BMW dealership lot in my truly beautiful 3 series BMW, which I had purchased off the showroom floor just two years prior. It was a blast of a car. Sleek and elegant yet smaller than the 5 series. If you do not know this yet, let me inform you that the number 5 is bigger than the number 3. In my mind, I processed this to mean that since 5 is bigger than 3, then 5 is better, and it would therefore make me to look better also. I knew I could afford it. *The dealer told me so.* (Side note: the dealer's role is not to be your friend or help you make wise financial choices. His role is to *sell* you a car. Be aware of this *fact* prior to your arrival.) He also told me that this 5 Series *"looked good on me"* and that when I drove up to meetings, they would know I was a *"serious businessman"* . . . Hahaha! Vanity and Pride. The ENTIRE time I test-drove it, I knew it was *not* the right car for me. I knew, but I accepted that if I could, that meant I should. I lived to regret that choice. I only had that car for approximately eight months. I named it the Albatross (a symbol of a bad choice or omen from *The Rime of the Ancient Mariner* by S. Coleridge). You see, although it *could* have been everything I wanted, it became a symbol of a choice that I *should* not have made . . . and I knew it.

So how do you know *when* and *when not* to make a move in life? Some situations are simple. If you do not have the money, do *not* buy it. If the person does not hold the same values as you, do *not* date them. If the job will require you to compromise your beliefs, do *not* take it. When you know, you just know.

In the other 90 percent of decisions you will need to make, when the lines are not so clear, that's where *faith* becomes so important. I have found that by praying over the decisions in my life, I can always have *Peace* and *Clarity*. On the opposite, when I have ignored the direction(s) that I knew came from God or when I moved forward without *Peace*, I have lived to regret it. I have found that no possible outcome, no matter how lucrative, is worth pursuing without *Peace*. Just because you can have it or them doesn't mean you should.

#3

THINK BEFORE YOU SPEAK.
WORDS MATTER.

"The average man thinks about what he has said. The above average man thinks of what he will say." These very true words have been attributed to Daniel Webster, the creator of *Webster's Dictionary*.

Have you ever been around someone that talks before they think? A friend who constantly puts their foot in their mouth? So, you already understand the problems it can cause. Friendships are destroyed. Relationships are broken. Drama is created. And all this because someone rattles off a word from their lips before they take a moment to process its impact. We often forget that words spoken in a moment can take years to repair. This is why the Bible states that "*Life* and *Death* are in the *Power* of the tongue."

If there is both life and death in these little words we often so carelessly toss around, then why spend no time pondering their effect or value before spewing them out? While they can have the destructive force of a weapon, we treat words with no long-term significance.

But I believe if we are honest with ourselves, we actually know this already. Within our heart and *mind*, we are aware of this tool of demolition; yet in the moment of frustration, hurt, or anger, we choose to separate from restraint and "let slip the dogs of war," resulting in carnage within our life and scaring those within our radius.

Which leads to the question, who will you restore or tear down today? What dreams will you build or destroy today? Will you be wise in what you say, or will you verbally become part of the problem? The choice is yours to think or not think before you speak.

Abraham Lincoln once wrote, *"A drop of honey catches more flies than a gallon of gall."* It's astonishing the effect of a kind word over a harsh remark. It can end wars, restore the spark of life, and even change a destiny.

So then, with this knowledge in our minds, the song of my childhood still rings true, "be careful little tongue what you say," for the impulsive words of a moment can very well carry consequences for a lifetime. Speak *Life*, not death. Just a thought . . .

"The one who has knowledge uses words with restraint, and whoever has understanding is even-tempered. Even fools are thought wise if they keep silent, and discerning if they hold their tongues" (Proverbs 17:27–28).

MAKE NO PROMISE YOU CANNOT KEEP.

Too often we make agreements before we have completely processed the request. It's easy to say in a moment, "I've got your back" or "I'm with you." In our culture, we commonly use words like *forever* when what we really mean is right now. We have forgotten that the agreements and commitments we make, both written and verbal, have authority and power. And too often, we enter agreements before we consider the weight of the consequences, whether good or negative. We as a culture no longer consider that our "word is our bond" (meaning an actual contract). We have been lied to and deceived so that too often, truth is interpreted as relative to the situation rather than an unchanging fact. This perception will never change unless it starts with you. Your word must matter. It must matter to your family, your friends, your classmates, your associates, and eventually to your children. Words matter, and those around you must know that your word is your bond. That if you say it, you mean it. The only way things will ever change is if it starts with you. Before you say you will do something, consider the weight of your promise. After all, *Words Matter*!

#5

GUARD YOUR HEART.

Is it any wonder that the wise old King penned in Proverbs 4:23, to do this "above all else"? He was wealthy above all others, he was respected by his people, he had a massive kingdom, and he had a gorgeous wife (actually, he had over three hundred of those . . . but that's another story . . .), but he still stated to "Guard your Heart" as the Highest standard for living.

It really is a wonder how we live our lives with our hearts "open," without guard, to the words and influences of everyone around us. Is it any wonder that heartbreak is a constant in adolescent relationships? Prior to truly getting to know someone, we too often open our hearts to words like *love*, which often generates unprocessed emotions and, in many teen relationships, turns into a physical sexual response. Then when these relationships come apart, our unguarded hearts endure trauma, which leaves scars. I believe this is why we call it heartbreak. In our American culture, we have become addicted to the thought of love and the idea of physical intimacy, yet we do not put any focus on the damage that occurs when things go bad.

We also must choose to guard our heart from the words of others. I cannot tell you how many times I have counseled young men or women who were broken, and often depressed, due to the careless or malicious words of someone they called friend. Even as a kid, I would hear the phrase "sticks and stones may break my bones but words will never hurt me," but that is possibly the biggest of lies.

Words do hurt. They can punch as hard as any fist and leave a bruise that lasts a lifetime.

So then, how do I suggest that we protect ourselves from relationships that could go bad or from words that could hurt deep? Am I suggesting that you completely isolate yourself from anyone and everyone that could potentially hurt you? Absolutely not.

However, what I am suggesting is that we do not open ourselves up to just anyone. We must set standards and have expectations of those we are in a relationship with, whether romantic or friendship. If we begin to see the signs that they do not truly care for us, our feelings or ultimately our heart; then we must reconsider the future of that relationship, which could save us a lot of heartache.

The next important part of guarding your heart is in your response after you are hurt by someone and the damage is done. Too often, when we are wounded, we internalize the pain. It begins to fester like a wound, and as it gets infected, we become angry and often bitter. If we do not guard our heart, it will then become entangled in that bitter infection, thereby doing even more damage to us than the original injury.

If it is true that all the outcomes of my life will flow from my heart, then allowing hurt to remain could have a catastrophic outcome. That is why King Solomon gave counsel to his children to guard their hearts so carefully. Now that you know, the hardest part will be to live this out, but it is possible. You can live a life of peace, forgiveness, hope, joy, and true love, but only if you choose to guard your heart.

#6

THINK BEFORE YOU DO.
LIVE WITH A LONG-TERM
PERSPECTIVE.

When I was sixteen, I wanted a tattoo. It was the thing to do, and I thought I should have one. My parents were completely against the idea of getting a tattoo, but as a teenager/young man, I just wanted what I wanted, regardless of the consequences. When I went off to college at eighteen, I figured it was time to get one since I was an "adult," and my roommate had one. At that time, vintage cartoon characters were very popular. Mickey Mouse was everywhere. One friend had a Yosemite Sam tattoo and another friend had a Speedy Gonzales on his leg. In my young mind, I thought Mickey would be a great tat . . .

Pretty funny, right? Fortunately, I was unable to afford that purchase. Now as an adult in my thirties, I cannot imagine how horrible it would be to have a cartoon figure Permanently on my body. My perspective has changed. What once was young and fun would now be embarrassing and ridiculous. My tattoo scenario is laughable, I know, but how often do we make *permanent* decisions based on temporary desires? Too often we go rushing into relationships, agreements, and contracts based on current attraction or quick solutions rather than taking the time to pray or seek wise counsel. Then we are often left with years of pain and struggles as a result of the consequences of our actions. This is why it is so very important to think before you do. Prior to that next date, meeting, contract, job opportunity, or move, process if it's the right move for your life . . . in five years . . . in ten or twenty? Although many decisions are not truly clear till years later, many bad choices can be averted if you will process through the possible consequences first; seek wise counsel, and I personally always pray also.

If you don't think before you do, then you'll live a life thinking about what you should have done . . . and that is *no* way to live. Think *Long*-term.

#7

PRODUCE MORE THAN
YOU CONSUME.

The United States as a whole has become a *Nation* of *Consumers*. The fundamental principle of all lasting *Wealth* is "Produce more than you consume" and then to sell it to those who will purchase and consume what you have produced. If you do this, there will always be a "Need" for more than you will ever *Produce*. This is the basis of supply and demand, so why do we not teach this principle of success? The fact is most individuals do not apply this principle into their everyday decisions and life goals, which is why most individuals are not achieving their goals and living their dreams. Interested in being different than the norm?

Good. Then how can you apply this to your daily living? I'm glad you asked. Here are a few suggestions that I have added into my life.

First, *Build something*. For me, I built, with God's help, a few companies. After much prayer and with a lot of motivation, I struck out on the entrepreneurial journey to create a couple of companies that met a need for individuals who became my clients, which provided an income for our employees and generated revenue for my family's financial needs. This did not happen because I was brilliant or especially gifted but rather because I listened to God. I was driven and knew I had a purpose. I knew there was a need within me to build something bigger then me in my community. You must find what you were created to build, and once you do, you will produce something great for your family and for society as well.

Second, *Grow something.* When I was growing up, I helped my Pop plant a large garden on our land every spring. There was something special about putting food on our table, which we had grown by our own efforts. Even now, each year my children and I plant a large garden at our home. Often, we produce so many vegetables that we cannot eat them all, so we share them with our neighbors. Although I could go to the grocery store and purchase my veggies there, there is something uniquely special still about building a salad from our garden. Even as I'm writing this in the middle of winter, I wish I could run out to the garden right now and pick a salad! I am inspired that this desire to plant is growing among many your age with the sprouting up of urban and community gardens throughout our cities. Even if you do not have a space to plant a garden, I would suggest that this spring, you begin to grow a plant or two of your own. Tomato plants are a great place to start by the way. I truly believe you will be astonished and inspired by the feeling you get the first time you harvest something for your table that you yourself have produced. Just a thought . . .

Third, *Give something.* Although I have committed an entire chapter to giving, I still feel the need to mention it here. There is something amazing that you will find begins to produce in your life when you choose to give. Whether it is giving financially or of your time, giving always produces and never consumes. It produces hope in others because they see that someone cares. It produces inspiration in some because they then choose to give themselves. Giving also produces joy in your own life. Simply put, giving produces giving.

And with all that said, do not merely live a life of consuming, but rather produce something amazing for others and yourself. What you produce in others or in products could be the innovation that changes your world or others.

TRUST IN GOD MORE THAN YOU RELY ON YOURSELF.

The greatest struggle of any person's life is to trust in the Creator that he cannot see in the middle of circumstances that he does not understand. But it is in these times of dark places such as pressure, confusion, struggle, loss, and hurt that you see where you stand and in whom you will trust. It is in these most difficult seasons in life that you can grow to depend on Him. If not, I fear you will find yourself in an even darker place because the *Only* remedy for darkness is *Light*, and the only cure for doubt is *Faith*.

With that set as our foundation, the challenge moves to not living dependent upon our own strength. Too often, in these dark places, we resolve that we must fix the issues ourselves . . . with our own strength and wisdom. We toil. We dig deeper. We work harder. We struggle more and more, believing that if we can just give enough, we can be our solution provider. When we temporarily patch the issue and gain relief, we develop an even deeper dependency upon ourselves. Then when our struggles do not produce the result we had hoped for, we become even more disillusioned, which often leads to greater blame. And yet all this can be resolved by placing our *Faith* not in ourselves but rather in the Creator, for in Him we will find the answers, solutions, hope, and peace that we so desperately want and need.

What does that look like? Glad you asked! So, the next time you are facing an issue in your life, *stop* and ask for God's help and guidance. Seems simplistic, I know, but it's a place to start, and I have found that every journey begins with the first step. Then throughout the choices and struggles of each day, talk to God about them. Ask Him for His best for your life. Sometimes you will feel like you have an answer and other times you might not. Once again, in those times, you can learn to *Trust* in God rather than yourself. I challenge you to try Him today. It starts with a step.

#9

RESPECT OTHERS AND GIVE OTHERS A REASON TO RESPECT YOU.

In our modern Western society, we have this notion that "respect is earned," implying that respect is all about the recipient. Although it is true that each of us should make great effort to "earn" the respect of others through purchase, words, and actions, I contend that respect is a *Choice* and is *Given* above all. While it is true that respect has been earned by those who have fought for our Nation or paid a great price to protect and serve society, we often see examples where those individuals still did not receive the respect they had rightfully earned. I believe this is caused because of a major misunderstanding of what *Respect* is in our modern Western world.

First off, *Respect* comes with *Age*.

Simply put, respect your elders. They really do know more than you do. They have walked farther on this life journey than you have, and that alone merits respect. Along with age also comes wisdom, which equally merits respect. If we fail to identify their wisdom and give the respect they are due, this can also result in lost potential for us since we will not be position to gain from their wisdom. This can be truly tragic! So always respect your elders. They just might hold the key the unlocks the door to your dreams and *future*.

Secondly, *Respect* comes with *Consistency*. We've all been around those associates who live life with the "fake it till you make it" philosophy. One day they are of one opinion and the next they're on the complete opposite end of the spectrum. They jump from job to job to job and never complete anything. They are unstable in all their ways. It is very difficult to respect someone like that. By their lifestyle, they make it challenging. However, while we as individuals must operate with a *Consistent* mind-set that produces a sense of respect toward us by others, we must *Choose* to find positive traits in those who live inconsistent lives and respect them for those traits. After all, for those of us who lead, respect is more about you giving than about others earning it.

Thirdly, *Respect* comes with *Action*.

Sometimes we will not be "liked" because of our actions. As a conservative, I believe that certain situations' actions and choices are wrong arena that are destructive for individuals and their families. When I voice those opinions, it can often result in me being polarizing and unpopular with those who do not share my views. Although I believe as a Christian that I must always show love through all my actions, I equally believe that I must be honest in those beliefs even when it's not popular with my friends and those around me. In life, if you choose to speak and *act* based on your beliefs, there will be many times when you will be disliked for it. In those times, that's when it will be the most difficult to remain consistent, but that's why your actions are so important. If your actions, through love, consistently reflect who you are and what you believe, people will eventually respect you for them . . . even if they do not agree. A dear friend of mine who has operated in the political field for many years once told me a motto that he had learned from a mentor. The thought goes *"Be Loved by some and Hated by others, but be Respected by all."* I'm the type of person who wants to be liked! So, when my friend John first told me this, I struggled with it, like you might be right now. But this motto simply means in life, you will have some individuals who naturally like you and others that dislike you for whatever reason, whether substantiated or not. But if you live your life in a consistent and respectable manner, you can create a lifestyle for which all individuals who know you will respect you. But in honesty, if you live a consistent life of action through love based on your beliefs and don't just change with whatever fad modern culture is on, you will be hated, or at least disliked, at some point for your principles. But if you continue to walk it out, you will eventually be respected by those individuals regardless . . . and I personally will take respect over being popular any day of the week!

So, in the end, *respect* others and *live* a life worthy of the respect of others. Both are a *Priceless* investment.

#10

THE COMPANY YOU KEEP IS THE BRAND YOU'LL WEAR.

Proximity to success will ultimately influence your environment. I call this your *Proximity of Environment*. If you spend your time with bitter or negative people, before long your words will become like poison and your dreams will eventually die. If you hang around four broke guys, you will eventually be the fifth. Should you surround yourself with individuals who say "You can't . . .," then simply put, you won't. Our environment and relationships determine so much of what we will achieve, because what they say and do eventually will become what you will believe you can achieve.

That is why it is often necessary to change your environment and even relocate yourself prior to seeing things change. We see this throughout society. Good kid put in a bad school ends up with bad results as a dropout working a minimum wage job while the same kid given a chance at a better educational environment thrives and succeeds going on to university earning a degree. Environment is half the battle.

If you're struggling with doubt, get around some people of *Faith*. If you're struggling with fear, surround yourself with courageous people who have faced some *Giants* themselves. If you're needing a healing, spend some time with someone who's received theirs! It's not rocket science. In the words of the wise old King, "As a man thinketh, so is he" (Proverbs 23:7). *So too, as a man surrounds himself, so will he become.* So, begin to consider who you call your friends today and where you plan to hang out tonight. Your tomorrow very likely depends upon it.

SPEND LESS THAN YOU MAKE.

This rule seems like a "no-brainer," but the majority of Americans do not abide by it. Consumer debt (unsecured or credit card debt), is literally a financial cancer that eats the life out of American households and is growing daily. Some studies show that *financial* stress is the *number one reason for divorce in America*, sighting as much as 57 percent! In honesty, *Debt* is a destroyer and should be avoided at all costs. In addition, social media and reality TV have created an incubator that breeds constant examples of "*what we do not have that others do.*" Throughout the day, images of expensive cars, jewelry, clothes and houses are *Constantly* displayed to remind us of what we do not have. If allowed to plant in our minds, this viewing can quickly turn to coveting, which turns to envy, that becomes bitterness, and eventually hate once it plays out. The worst part of this destructive "need for what I don't have" is found in our lack of appreciation for what we already have and a corrosive desire to *get it* at any cost . . . even if I must go into debt to get it! If you decide to live a life such a life, enough will *Never* be enough and *Debt* will rule your FUTURE! Scary, right? It should be.

So then, how will we "get what we want"? In a word: *Save.* Now I realize the idea of saving is not exciting. There is nothing fun about it. It is not a concept that people brag about at dinner parties or at work or around the lunch table. However, it is a habit that can change your life, your future, and your family tree. By spending less than you make, you can begin to put back money into savings to acquire *what you want.* By delaying your purchase, you can pay for it in cash . . . thus not going into debt and compromising your future.

Just consider this thought. If you worked a job in high school or college, saving $400 to $500 per month ($100 to $125 per week) for ten months, you could purchase yourself a $4,000 to $5,000 car with cash. That's a really decent car that could last you for a couple of years. Now let's say during those two years you continue to work and save that same amount per month, you could be sitting on $10,000 within a couple of years! Now, if you have saved, as I'm suggesting, you have an account with around $10,000 and a car that is still worth $3,000 to $4,000. If you now want a newer car, you could sell your current one, take that $3,000 to $4,000 and add $3,000 or $4,000, which would position you to purchase a $6,000 to $8,000 car while leaving you still with $6,000 to $7,000 in your savings . . . . Plus *no Debt*! Now I know I'm thinking crazy here, but what if you continued to *pay yourself* (instead of an auto dealer/Loan) from now on? That account after just ten years would be enough to purchase a house . . . in Cash. Or if you continue to save that same amount monthly, invest it in a solid growth mutual fund (I would suggest something with a track record of 12 percent annual return), and remain consistent, you could retire as a *Multi-Millionaire*—all because you decided to *Save* and pay *Cash* for your *Cars*! That's the power of *Consistent Saving* and *Compound Interest*! Just that one change from the "normal" can change your family tree, and it all begins by spending less than you make. Save for the *Future* you want!

#12

ALL YOU OWN IS YOUR RESPONSE.

Throughout the years, I cannot count how many times I have spoken with individuals who are hurt and broken by the actions of others, but they feel the need to fix the other person's actions. Too often, after being done wrong by someone close to us, we think it is our responsibility, whether consciously or subconsciously, to *help* them *do better*. Unfortunately, this seems to never go well. We could just as easily turn the tide of the ocean as change the actions of someone else. In honesty, until they are ready to change, there is no amount of help you can give that will ever make a difference. So then, what do we do?

First off, *try always to do the right thing even when the wrong thing seems right*. This principle has served me well throughout life. When someone does us wrong and causes us hurt, our instinct is to retaliate. As the saying of old goes, *an eye for an eye*. But when we live our life in this way, it will always result in causing more pain. One hurt causes another wound, which results in another offense . . . it becomes an endless cycle of agony. However, if we instead positioned our hearts to let go of offense, not only will we release the offender of our judgment, we will actually find freedom for ourselves. It is in the liberation of the *culprit of our pain* that we find the peace our Creator desires for our expedition of life. Even if this seems wrong in the moment, by doing the right thing, we position ourselves for the life of freedom we desire.

Secondly, *All you own is Your Response.* You cannot choose how people will treat you or speak about you. You cannot change your past either or the transgressions (wrongdoings) that even those closest to you have committed against you. You do not own their actions or their lack of an expression of regret. That's on them, not *you.* There broken inability or flawed choices to not repent is their burden, not *yours.* All you own is how you respond to it. Although each of us desire for the causer of our scar(s) to pay penance for their infractions, we often are seeking a justice that a judgment cannot deliver. In truth, your response to the wound will determine your outcome much more so than the verdict of public opinion. So rather than seeking to execute them in the halls of social viewpoints, for the sake of your own heart, you must choose to guard your heart and the response it produces.

I understand that such a thought is not only difficult but it is absolutely abnormal. And not only is such advice unusual, but it is even insanely undesirable in our modern culture . . . yet it is a true path to freedom and can release you from the bondages of a vengeful heart. No, it will not be easy. Some days it will test you to your core, but if you will get your eyes off the offenses that others have distressed you with and choose to respond with a liberated heart, in my experience, you will find joy greater than your burdens, producing a life of liberty. Choose to not live in the chains of the actions of others but do the *right* thing and own your *response.*

#13

READ ABOUT TODAY WHAT YOU WANT TO DO TOMORROW.

Media. Media. Media. Nonstop. Constant streaming visual media—24/7. Never ending. If you want, you can download or stream videos on any subject any time of day, which has made the ability to learn about a subject quick and fairly easy. If I want to take a thirty-minute course on applied physics, I can put the app on my phone and *increase my understanding* in less time than it takes to drive to a library. Let's say I want to get an *overview* of Shakespeare's *Hamlet* for a test tomorrow morning, there is a fifteen-minute video to solve that problem. Media, through the Internet, has allowed anyone almost anywhere to have access to education on almost *any* subject almost instantly. That's a lot of *almost*! How could that *possibly* be bad? Why would I *ever* want to pick up a book again??

For starters, did you know that some studies show that your brain makes cognitive "maps" with the information that you read, allowing you to connect the new information with previously learned details? In other words, it helps you get *smarter quicker* by connecting what you didn't know with what you do know as a result of reading the words. Another unfortunate side effect of a *CliffsNotes* society is the lack of depth of knowledge on a subject. Let's take Shakespeare's *Hamlet* as a working example. If I merely do an Internet search, read one of the "Hamlet for Numb-Skulls" type of books or just watch the movie, I miss out on the deep well of thought-provoking questions that the young prince ask as he faces the conflict of his mother marrying his uncle, who is now king, all while grieving the death of his father—and I thought my family had issues! But if I do not read it, so much is lost in the brief translation of this famous sixteenth-century play, which in its original form cast light onto the background of many current movies, TV shows, and songs. While that was an example, I realize most of us do not care to commit the time necessary to digest the four-thousand lines of Shakespeare's longest work. However, it does affect our daily lives and dreams for tomorrow in a very real way because *Books are your greatest accessible resource for learning HOW to accomplish your dreams and goals.*

Regardless of your life ambition, whether it's to be an entrepreneur, a veterinarian, a singer, a professional athlete, a great parent, an astronaut, a preacher, or the President of the United States, there is a *Book* about it, *and* there is likely a book by someone who already reached that dream! You see, *I view the author of each book I read as a Mentor.* Although I cannot sit in the room with many of my professional heroes, I can learn from their experiences, challenges, and successes from their written words. I can find inspiration from their struggles and hope from their triumphs. I can grow in intellect, increasing the strategies to meet my life goals by researching their systems they used to navigate turbulent times in their position . . . increasing the chances that I will not fall into the same pit, but providing a map if I should. I now personally have committed to read five books at a time, with a goal of not just skimming but completely reading fifty books a year. It is a lot, but I have *a lot* of dreams and goals to accomplish! *The larger the dream, the greater the need for knowledge.* In other words, what you read about today can help determine what your future will be. Books can be your greatest resource for accomplishing you dreams or goals. So, simply put, pick up a book. Learn. Grow. Prepare. Take the time to *Read. Your Dreams Depend on it!*

#14

HOLD THE DOOR FOR A STRANGER AND ALWAYS OPEN THE DOOR FOR A LADY.

You can tell a lot about a person by their normal, everyday actions. Once upon a time in our nation, we had a belief that a man should "be a gentleman," and he should "always respect a lady." Somewhere along the time line, such a notion became old-fashioned and out of date. Somewhere between music videos, movies, reality TV, and tasteless music—all which demean women and reduce them down to objects for male entertainment the nobler self of chivalry was reduced to a black and white TV show that our grandparents watched long ago. But this is a false belief. This concept of being a gentleman or a lady has just as much place in your success today as it did a century ago . . . possibly even more since there are less examples of it, thus allowing you the opportunity to shine even brighter. Still not convinced? Consider this example:

If you are walking toward an exit, if the person in front of you keeps going and let's go of the door as they pass through, it will likely give you the opinion that that individual is rude and inconsiderate. Although they very well might not intend to be rude by nature, their unthoughtful action implies it. What can be concluded factually, however, is that the individual, in that specific moment, is consumed by themselves and the situation that they are in. Although by nature, they might typically be a very considerate individual, in that moment, because of whatever is happening in their life, they at best have compromised their good character because they are focused more on their situation than being courteous to their fellow man.

You can also tell a lot about the character of a man by how he treats the ladies in his life. Too often, because of "societal change in gender roles," young men get the impression that opening a car door or holding the door for lady is no longer necessary. I would, however, like to debunk such a sentiment. It quite possibly is even more important today than ever for your success in meeting the right person and accomplishing your goals. You see, when there this a shortage of *anything*, it makes that item or action rare. Any commodity or behavior that is scarce becomes exponentially more valuable to those who desire it. Now, ladies, you should always expect a man to open your door. Why? Because it is an outward sign of his inward chivalry and intentions. If he does not even have the decency to make the effort to show such a small courtesy, you can have very little hope that he will ever be the kind of man you would want to spend a considerable amount of time with, much less marry and live your life with. Old-fashioned? Maybe. But ask yourself why many of the couples who are in their nineties have been married for seventy-plus years while over 50 percent of couples who say their vows now get divorced within two years . . . Now consider which group you would rather be in? It all starts with an act of kindness and mutual respect. If you are not willing to start on such a foundation, do yourself a favor and *do* not waste your time until you are ready. Either way, Gentlemen, act like it. Be valiant and chivalrous. Be kind and use good manners. It will always pay off in *life*. And, Ladies, be polite and expect a young man to be a Gentleman. If he's not, *Move On*!

Since I realize this is VERY old-school way of thinking, I'm sure I have challenged a few of you and likely I have inflamed one or two of you to absolute anger. But I must pose the question, if you find the thought offensive for a young man to be a gentleman and to hold the door open, why? Would it not make the world a better place if we all cared more about the well-being of others more so than ourselves and reflected such actions by chivalrous choices? I personally believe it would. So, I must recommend that you choose to live your life in such a caring way and expect it of those you choose to surround yourself with. But this is Just a thought . . .

15

WEAR A TIE TO AN INTERVIEW.

In my early twenties, I moved to a new city to return to college. Although I had some support from my family, I needed income to cover my bills. I "searched" for a couple of months with little luck and drained most of my savings. I heard of a job at a large retail store, but I felt working for that company was "beneath" me. After a "pep talk" (reminder) from my parents, I decided to at least interview with the company. I sat in a room with seventy other applicants, most were older than me and all applying for the same few jobs. After an online test and an initial one-on-one interview, something different happened for me. While the rest of the applicants were released, I was asked to stay behind. Next, another person came in to ask me questions, followed by another, and then another. What happened next, I must admit, although confident, I did not expect to happen. A man in a well-starched white dress shirt with a strong tie walked into the room. He sat and asked me five questions before leaving the room. When he returned, he brought in two of the previous interviewers, and they offered me a job. I went in applying for a cart pusher or cashier position, but that's not what I was offered. They asked me if I would like a midmanagement position instead making $2 more per hour than the other positions. I accepted, of course, and began my management journey working my way up through three promotions over the next two years. When I left that company to accept a higher-paying salary position for another company, I was managing over three hundred employees, and the point of sell for one of the largest stores in the company. Did I mention I was a full-time college student at that time? Before I left my position at the retail giant, I asked the man that wore the finely pressed white dress shirt with the strong tie who hired me why he gave me a chance that day. Out of all the other hundreds of applicants, why did he offer me a position as a manager? He said something that has stuck with me all these years since. "*You wore a tie.*" He went on to say that not only was I the only person that day to dress up, but I was the only one to ever wear a tie for a nonmanagement interview. The ONLY one . . . How many opportunities were lost by qualified or talented or driven individuals *because they did not dress for what they wanted more than what they expected?*

I went on from that position to a salaried management position with a large pharmaceutical company where I worked for a few years before founding my first company when I was twenty-six. From there, I have been blessed to start multiple companies, which has allowed me the opportunity to serve as a community leader, public speaker, a youth pastor, a business teacher, an author—blah blah blah . . . In other words, that one choice can be directly correlated to much of what I am grateful for in business. So, if I may, I would recommend looking your best the next time you go to fill out an application or a job interview. It just might make all the difference. It sure can't hurt. Just a thought . . .

#16

THINK CHESS, NOT CHECKERS.

As a child, I learned how to play checkers. Since it is a fairly simple game, I was able to pick up on the rules quickly. With single jumps and the objective of taking the opponent's pieces before he could take mine, a lot of cognition was never required. Everything in checkers is about this jump . . . or double jump if you are lucky, but little in regards for the next three moves. Honestly, although it requires some thought, for the most part, checkers is not a game of strategy. Through my experience, this is how the majority of individuals live their life. If they want a different car, they will go out and finance the most expensive thing on the lot for the smallest payment possible while not taking into consideration the *interest* rate they will be financing or the number of months it will take them to pay it off. For this same reason, people will quit a job or walk out of a position without notice or the commitment of other employment. Most of society think "instant gratification" with a throw-it-into-the-microwave mentality or run-through-the-drive-through concept of decision making. They want what they want, and they want it right *now*, regardless the long-term cost. This is why many of our family and neighbors live paycheck to paycheck, with just enough to barely get by. This philosophy of living guides every area of their lives. Financ e. Employment. Relationships. And unfortunately, many times, this shortsightedness leads to bankruptcy in all of these areas.

Now compare checkers with chess. Although they share an identical board, the goal is very different. In chess, the goal is not to take whatever jump that is set before you (as in checkers) but rather to accomplish the goal of taking the opponent's king, which we call "checkmate." Regardless of how much time it takes or the number of pieces the opposition has left on the board or even if the queen, bishops, knights, and castles are all taken or untouched . . . there is a solitary goal of placing the king in *checkmate*, and all this requires *strategy*. In chess, part of one's strategy can be to "sacrifice" pieces. In much the same way, in *life* we MUST make sacrifices if we desire to succeed. Also in chess, the current move is more about the next three or four moves, rather than *instantly* winning or getting the desired solution. I have found that one of the best strategies to increase my probability of winning is to sacrifice a key piece, such as a bishop or castle. As I draw the opponent into seeing the perceived accomplishment of the moment, I set him up for a crushing defeat through the distraction.

This method of strategy is why many in our culture are cash poor. They are playing a game of "instant gratification," *get-it-now* checkers with companies and individuals who are playing "long-term strategy," *slow-and-steady-wins-the-race* chess. While the majority want it (the car, house, vacation, etc.) right now, those with the financial means are dangling what the majority want on a string of *long-term, high-interest* DEBT. Frankly, it's a brilliant strategy. However, *you* do not need to play the wrong game. You and your family can be different, but only if you know the rules of the game and determine to not participate in the "poor man's game."

Will this be difficult? Sometimes, *very* difficult! You will have friends (associates) who post about their NEW job, car, house, relationship, vacation, or whatever, which will make you think that yours is not as good as theirs. Now you want one like theirs—or *Better*! So, you will ask yourself, "Don't I deserve it?!" Convinced of the *injustice* of them having one, you can quickly justify that you too *deserve* one . . . so, you can get it! But *only* if you choose to play checkers instead and thereby jeopardize this idea. Will you want to just "be normal" like everyone else who is up to their eyeballs in debt? I hope not! Because debt *Bites* . . . often literally! So, set your *Goals* that you desire to achieve in both this *season* of your life and long-term. Then set a budget. Live by your *budget*. Fight for your *budget*. Live below your means! That means spend LESS than you make. If you do so, you will always have extra to *save* for the rainy days ahead.

Once you have these ideas working for you, then you can begin the strategies to succeed in life. Your steps will be ordered not just not just for today or tomorrow but for next year and the next ten years to follow. By living a life thinking about your next ten steps, you can position yourself for the "long game." Fight for real success . . . not just a temporary win. Dream big today, but live by a budget and a plan. After all, a *goal* without a plan is merely a wish. Live a life of *strategy*. Think *chess*.

The 90% Principle.

As an entrepreneur, 90 percent of what you do to build a successful venture will not be seen. However, this 90 percent is the foundation and structure that will support the 10 percent that your clients will identify as your company and love (or hate, depending on the 90 percent). The hidden 90 is crucial to all you desire to achieve. I am equally of the opinion that this principle holds true for education as well. It is the 90 percent of your time in studying, preparation, and training that prepares you for the title or position you desire to hold. Thus, I believe your success is dependent upon the unseen 90 percent. Just a thought . . .

#18

GIVE.

There is something amazing that you will find begins to produce in your life when you choose to give. Whether it is, giving financially or of your time, giving *always produces* and *never consumes*. It produces hope in others because they see that someone else cares and it sets the example for them to then mimic. Even a child can understand the concept of giving, and by seeing others experience joy in their own lives, it sets a desire in their hearts to not live selfishly but to give of themselves. There's nothing more fulfilling than unselfish or sacrificial giving, whether monetarily or of your time. Simply put, giving produces giving, and it feels really good to share!

We've often heard the saying, "Give until it hurts," but I believe you should *"Give until it feels good"*! This is a great principle to live by for *true* success also! In fact, every truly successful individual or *corporation* I have had the privilege of associating with, one consecutive trend is always found in their extravagant generosity. On a personal level, the biggest reward will be the joy that springs up in your own life as a result of giving. It is also important for you to remember, *Giving is what you do;* **Generosity is part of who you are**. So, who will you choose to be? My recommendation . . . *Be a giver and Live Generously.*

#19

SEIZE THE DAY AND LIVE IN YOUR MOMENT.

Too often in my life, I've lived at the speed of *life*. Many times, in the middle of some of the most extraordinary experiences surrounded by exceptional individuals, I have found myself so busy attempting to get the perfect picture to post on social media that I have missed truly connecting, seeing, or learning from exposure to the location or event. Rather than living in the moment and "taking it all in," I was too consumed with projecting the *idea of it* by posting to show where I was to individuals who were not even part of that experience! In other words, I was more concerned about what others thought than connecting with the very people I was there with in the first place . . . Sounds a little insane, doesn't it? And yet this is the *Normal* for this generation in modern society. Constant consuming social media "friends" rather than intimate focused relationships. I believe we must personally break this cycle. It starts by putting down the phone and pursuing real connections. The next time you are at the table, put away your device. The next time you are standing on a mountain with friends trying to get the perfect selfie, wait till later to post it so you can stay connected with those you are with presently. Do not live in desperation to share what you're doing at the expense of spending time with who you are with. Make each moment count.

The other danger of distraction is seen in missing one's moment. After all, distraction is a destroyer of dreams. As you have read these thoughts of mine, I'm sure you have noticed by now that

I love quotes. One of my favorite gentlemen to recite is Sir Winston Churchill, who once said, *"There comes a special moment in everyone's life, a moment for which that person was born. That special opportunity, when he seizes it, will fulfill his mission- a mission for which he is uniquely qualified. In that moment, he finds greatness. It is his finest hour."* But consider if when that moment knocks upon the door of life, you are distracted. The *he* or *she* of your dreams walks right up next to you at the counter to order an overpriced coffee beverage, but you do not notice because you are busy socially stalking someone you have not even spoken to in years. Possibly, you are invited to a lunch but you cannot attend because your dog is sick or you could not sleep last night (a.k.a.: because you stayed up all night playing video games, etc.), which results in you not meeting an associate of theirs who holds the key to your first entrepreneurial startup. Maybe it's the last game of a losing season and you just decide to not show up, yet you do not know that today was your day to slam two over the right fence and catch the attention of the college scout, who was there to observe a player for the other team. You see our *life* is *Full* of these "And Then" moments. They are distinctively unrepeatable. These are those opportunities that you yourself cannot create but just by showing up and being present in the right moment, God opens a door where there had only been a wall. But you first MUST show up, be present in the *Moment* "And Then" you must Seize it!

Too often over the years of working with youth, college students, and business owners, I have witnesses many attempts to make deals with God. Often, we pray, "Lord, if you will supply, I will make the move." Yet I find that His response is often, "My Child, you make the move, and I will supply." You see, I believe *Opportunities* in the *Right Moment* must be *Seized*! I like that word: *Seize*. It means "to grab, to take hold of quickly." It states that the moment for waiting has ended and the opportunity is NOW. It reflects to *Horace's Odes* (I. 11), which shouts, "Carpe diem," which loosely translated proclaims "Seize the day." What a powerful thought. Seize this day. It implies to not wait for tomorrow but make movement today. It declares be present in this moment, in this hour, and seek the most in it. It proclaims that your future rightly depends upon your awareness of the importance of now. It is as thought God is saying, "Move now."

With that thought, I question how many dreams men never see fulfilled because they merely ask but do not pursue? They dream but they do not seize the moments presented, thereby existing in the gray of a never-ending mediocrity rather than stepping out into deep water, believing that God will split the water, make their feet to walk on the tide of a dream. or just give them the strength to be a really great swimmer through the seas of possibility. So, what dreams hide within you? What is it that drives you but you dare not voice to "friends" and certainly do not pursue for fear of failure? Whatever they are, although you might be scared, when the moment presents itself, pray first, verbalize it second, and *Go* after it as though your future depends upon it! Simply stated, in the moments you will face, *Focus on Today*, *Live* in each *Moment*, *Don't* live distracted, and most importantly, when your moment knocks . . . *Seize* it!

#20

FAIR IS A 'FOUR LETTER' WORD.

The concept of "Fair" is a corrosive concept because it falsely teaches us that we deserve something. The word *Fair* means that my experience should be the same as someone else's or that I should receive the same reward as they although our experience and efforts are not identical. Too often in our American society, we see examples of individuals who pitch fits and protest when they do not believe the circumstances or *rewards* they are given are as good as those of others.

The truth is, not everyone gets the contract, not everyone gets first place, and truthfully, not everyone gets a trophy. The reality is in order to achieve the most, we must strive the hardest of all . . . and sometimes even when we do, we still don't get the prize. There will be times when you are the best and you give them most and yet you still will not be recognized for it. In these moments, your true character and *grit* will be seen. It is in these times of living in the shadow that the *merit* of who you are and will be will be defined. No, it's not easy to go above and beyond and not be recognized for it; however, for those who endure, there is a greater prize. For in these moments of the *hidden* season, your resolve will be established. During these times of being unknown, you will be in preparation for everything you were created to be.

That is why many never make it to succeed and see their dreams come true. Instead of continuing in the process, they quit and scream "Unfair!" They choose to become bitter and complain about the lack of fairness in their life or situation. However, there are a few wood shoes to remain in the process, and for those few brave souls, we have a term that is also a four-letter word . . . *Hero*. So, what will your story be? When in the times when you are overlooked and feel forgotten and often betrayed, what will you choose to do? Will you remain in the process and allow your integrity to be built, will you remain committed to the cause you were created for? Will you choose to remain in the shadow with your conviction knowing that though the world may view it as unfair, your day will come for which you were born. Remain in the process. Just a thought . . .

#21

RUDENESS IS BENEATH YOU.

One thing I have learned from my time around the wealthy (the truly wealthy, built from generations of resource, not the quick-money first-generation group that is often reflected on TV reality shows or music videos) is they are not rude. They do not allow room for rudeness because they feel that it is beneath their ability to communicate. Although in our society, we often see poor examples portrayed in the headlines of gossip magazines, these individuals should not be the examples we strive to emulate (to act like or mirror). Instead, we should choose to act like actual royalty of a higher breeding. For those individuals, rudeness is thought to be common and unregal. For those raised in the lineage of kings and queens, to speak down to the lonely and hurting is thought to be beneath them.

So then why would we who are not of noble birth lower ourselves to such a diminished standard? Why would we ever attempt to hurt the heart of another human being to make ourselves feel bigger? Why would people such as us ever consider bullying another human with the expectation that we ourselves would feel larger?

So then, if we realize this type of life in tearing down others is beneath us, then we can not only choose for ourselves to lift others up, but we can also reflect that example to others around us. We can be resolute by lifting the hurting and the broken that cross our paths, knowing that by lifting them up, we create an environment that we can be lifted as well. For the truth is that not one will ever be lifted up who has not already lifted up others. So, the next time you feel like tearing down someone else, choose your words wisely and think twice. This may just be your opportunity to lift up one who needs it and might even prepare your for an opportunity of advancement. Don't live beneath. Lift others up.

#22

CHANGE WITH YOUR SEASON. ADAPT TO CHANGE.

Like it or not, seasons in life change, and we can adapt or be crushed by them. In honesty, this chapter may be the most difficult for me of this book. Like most, I am not a huge fan of change, at least not when things are comfortable or "good." On the contrast, when things are stressful or "bad," I find that I cannot wait for things to change! But whether we are ready for it or not, *Change* is *Constant* in our lives, and such is coming.

Since both "good" and "bad" change will be happening through-out the seasons of our lives, we must decide how to respond and adapt to these moments. It is essential that we process our response (as best we can) entering into these seasons; otherwise, our response might be only based in our momentary emotion. Processing our emotions and thoughts about a particular outcome can also help us to not live a roller-coaster life with drastic ups and downs. For me personally, I have found that *prayer* and meditating on scriptures from the Bible has been crucial in my process of working through difficult changes in life. The realization that I have found in these times is how, *momentary*, these struggles are for me. Although these circumstances are often excruciatingly painful at this instance, I have found through prayer along my journey that these sudden changes have strengthened my abilities and resolve more than any other assault. It is the detours along our path that not only stretch us but fortify our stamina for future conquest. After all, if we have no resistance, we will never develop the necessary strength required to defeat the future obstacles we must face to reach our dreams.

You will face changes, challenges, and losses. You are going to suffer defeats on your field of life. You will be knocked down, unjustly (and sometimes justly) fired, and sometimes your season will seemingly change overnight. One time on my business journey, I lost two companies in a matter of seventy-two hours . . . Yes, that one *Really Hurt!* But now, years removed from the sting, I can see how those losses developed me into the man I am today and closer to the man that God desires for me to become. It gashed my ambition at that time, but I would not exchange that experience now because I see the long-term effects now. What I thought would destroy me in that season actually is part of the foundation that I am currently constructing a much stronger corporation upon today. That *season* of loss positioned me for this *season* of gain.

So today, my child, you might be feeling pretty low because of a seemingly crushing breakup or loss of a job, but trust me in this . . . this is NOT the end of your story but rather a *New Beginning.* He or she simply was not the right one. That job was only a stepping stone on your street to the destination of success. One day, much like I have expressed in my story, you will look back knowing that this was merely a moment that repositioned you toward the divinely intended purposeful target. Just don't quit. When you are ready, dry your tears and accept the change. You will likely find that the path is greener up ahead as you move forward into your new season. Just a thought for your rainy days . . .

#23

DO NOT LIVE IN DRAMA.

Too often, people create problems for themselves or they allow others to dump problems on them. Like a backpack full of dirty diapers, the weight and stench of those problems follow them around. If we want to live peaceful and productive lives, we must *Refuse* to join the chaos. We must choose to not live burdened by such weights. Distance yourself from people and situations that breed drama. Exit the cycle of stress that "drama" and "dramatic people" perpetuate. Instead, *focus* on what needs to be done. Block out pointless words. Do not give in to pointless quarrels and arguments. Move forward and *Choose* to be free of drama. You will find that you live a more peaceful life when you do not entertain all the noise. Just a thought . . .

#24

KNOW WHAT YOU KNOW AND STAND ON IT.

I remember as a kid hearing a song by the country artist Aaron Tippin called "You've Got to Stand for Something." The ballad told the story of a father instructing his son with these words: "You've got to stand for something, or you'll fall for anything. You've got to be your own man, not a puppet on a string. Never compromise what's right and uphold your family name." This song reminds me of my Grandaddy, LeRoy Thornton. As a Pastor in the South, he faced many times when it would have been much easier to compromise his convictions, yet he knew who he was and stood for his beliefs. He taught me fundamentals like *"A man's word is his bond," "Let your Yes be Yes and your No be No,"* and to *"Do unto others as you want them do unto you."* His actions spoke volumes, and he lived a life that few could question. It was not easy, but doing the right thing rarely is unchallengeable. In fact, most of the time when you take a stand in your life, there *WILL* be a push back. It takes great strength to hold to your beliefs, especially when you feel like you are in the minority. During these times, you must guard your character and know (learn) the facts. That is why it is crucial to *Know* what you believe and *Stand* on it.

We currently live in a society that often bases value, principle, and *Truth* on whatever opinion poll, popular show, alternate lifestyle group, or in-demand artist has the largest megaphone. In a *world* that is constantly changing the views of right and wrong, it can be difficult to hold on to one's views of morality, especially when we feel pressure to go with "current wisdom" and to not be labeled as a *bigot, uneducated,* or *small minded.* However, if you do not stand for something, you literally will fall for anything.

So . . . what do you *know?* What do you *believe in?* On what mountain are you willing to take a stand?

Throughout your life, as you answer those questions, you must choose to not compromise your beliefs. Know what you know and Stand on it.

#25

BE FAITHFUL. LIVE COMMITTED.

Cheating and Quitting—few things can be more destructive in our everyday lives than these two responses to commitments. We have all seen broken family examples where one spouse just gave up on their vows and looked to another to find what they should have shared in their home. Each of us have either seen or felt the pain in a dating relationship when the boyfriend or girlfriend cheated. Examples of athletes who left a team for a bigger one fill the sports pages. Politicians who cheat on the public trust through crooked decisions and cover-ups stream across the news constantly. With all these instances of unfaithfulness and uncommitted lives displayed by those we put on a pedestal, it is no wonder that we are cynical about commitment as a society. Kind of seems hopeless, right? Well, it's *Not*! The greatest shame of all the brokenness left behind is it never would have happened had the unfaithful remained committed.

You see, *Commitment* still works, and it begins with a *Choice*. It starts when you choose to live dedicated to your *Faith* in God, your spouse, your beliefs, your family, or your cause. It commences when you decide that quitting or cheating is not an option. It continues every time you have the moment to compromise, yet you stand resolute in your convictions. And let me be honest, it will not always be easy to decline some of the offers you receive. There will be moments when you simply *want what you want*, and being unfaithful to what you know is right seems all right. Yet many times, the strength in our vows comes through talking the problem out. Our resolve is strengthened by spending quality dedicated time to building our *faith*, our relationship, our cause or career. It is in these moments of devotion that true conviction of principle develops and the core of who we are is solidified. *Simply stated, the more time you spend with who and what you love, the more you will Love them and it.* So, choose to live *Faithful* and *Committed Lives.*

#26

PEOPLE MATTER. NAMES MATTER.

I recently took my son to get a haircut at a new salon. It was a small location, but nice, clean, and well put together. As he was getting his trim, I began a conversation with the young lady whom I assumed to be the manager or owner. Over the next few minutes of discussion, I learned that she was the owner who had opened this new shop just a mere six months prior. Soon after we began speaking, my son's hair cut was complete, and we prepared to leave. As we were leaving, the owner shook my hand, shared her name, and asked my name. Nothing much, and then we were gone.

this young business and the shop she had created.

A few weeks later, I found myself in need of a fresh trim, so I decided to try the new salon where I'd taken my son. As I walked in without an appointment, I saw the owner and asked if they could fit me in today. That's when the unusual happened. As she looked at me to respond, she called me by my first name and then my last! This business owner had met me only once . . . on the one time I had taken my son to her business! I was completely and absolutely *Amazed*. I also felt "very important." Most importantly, I believed that I mattered to her business as a customer! I was so impressed, although they could not fit me in for an appointment then that I returned the following day to get my haircut. Also, that evening, as I taught a business class to a group of entrepreneurs, I raved about the *Excellence* of this young business owner and the unique effort she made in remembering me, thus securing my business! I was so impressed that I shared with the class that evening that I really hoped that she or her team would do good on my trim since she had won me as a client for life! All because she knew my name!

Although this might sound to be a little thing, there is proof that nothing secures the patronage of a client like feeling as though they matter. Consequently, nothing says you matter like someone knowing your name. In his groundbreaking book *How to Win Friends and Influence People*, Dale Carnegie states, "A man's name is to him the sweetest and most important sound in any language." He was so committed to that thought that he repeated it multiple times in his famous work. In truth, we all want to feel appreciated and to know that we matter to the other person and no basic ability reflects that more than in someone knowing your name.

Simply put, nothing evokes the VIP treatment like hearing one's own name, so stop making excuses and remember names. You just might find that by remembering theirs, they will remember yours at your greatest moment of need.

#27

LEARN TO IRON.

When considering the items that you will need to succeed on your own as an adult, for most, an Iron most likely does not make the top 10 list. However, it could quite possibly be the one appliance that can improve your chances of succeeding in an interview more so than any other household item. You see, more than the thread count or brand of shirt, the effort of properly pressing your attire reflects your commitment to both your personal and professional success. So why is it that an individual will spend $40 on a shirt to impress their interviewer when they would be much better serve spending $10 on a shirt and buying hey $15 iron and a bottle of starch? It's because we have a false perception of *true value*. What is even more unfortunate is the individual conducting the interview does not adhere to that same logic but rather couldn't care less the brand you're wearing while they will very much care about the appearance you project with a freshly starched garment. As an employer of hundreds over many years, I can attest that the individual who walks into the interview with a cleanly pressed wardrobe has ten times the opportunity of getting the job compared to the guy who did not even bother to iron.

So then, now that you know how to impress your potential employer, how are you supposed to properly iron your shirt? Well, I'm glad you decided to read this chapter! By my thinking, ironing is a form of art. Therefore, I so choose to explain it in a step by step method that should leave you with a perfectly pressed shirt or blouse.

The first step to successfully iron is to eliminate the areas that will not need to be touched back over. These are smaller sections like the collar and shoulders, which are unlikely to wrinkle throughout the rest of the ironing process. For me, I start with the collar. From there, I move to the shoulders because they also are unlikely to wrinkle again. Next you will move to the sleeves. Sleeves can be tricky because of their seams, which is why I always start in the bottom seam of the arm. From there, you can work your way in, that way you don't create more wrinkles as you go. Remember, smooth it out as you go, so you don't press over areas and accidentally create extra wrinkles. The other thing about sleeves is you must pay extra attention to the cuffs. A well-ironed cuff says a lot about a guy. Once your sleeves and cuffs are properly pressed, move to the back of the shirt. This is important because it is the largest area of your shirt that you will iron and you want to get it right. For me, I start on the left side and move to the right so I have a consistent flow. These things might seem incidental, but if you do them in the wrong order, then you end up with wrinkles on what you've already ironed. Which just creates more work and we do not believe in doing double work. Finally, move to the front of the item. I start with the side with the buttons, leaving the overlap as the last step. Take extra time and use extra starch on the front since this is the part that potential employers will see and notice. Let's not forget, the first impression makes all the difference!

FIND MENTORS.

Have you ever heard someone claim to be a "self-made" success? It produces mental images of a determined soul pressing alone against all odds to singlehandedly reach the heights of achievement . . . all alone . . . by his or her self. As arrogant as such a statement or thought is, it is equally absurd . . . and frankly impossible. In truth, no one can make it to the *Top* without the support or assistance of another. Whether it was the parent who took them to school, the teacher who gave them just a little more encouragement, the coach who pushed them past their previous goals, or even the friend who stood by them in the darkest hours of high school. Maybe it was the pastor, principal, employer, professor, neighbor, or classmate; but you can count on it—there was *Someone* who held their rope while they climbed to the top. No one makes it to the summit of the mountain alone.

If this is true, once you identify your "mountain," would it not make since then to find someone who has already made the journey and climbed to the top? It seems like it would be smart to seek advice from an individual who previously conquered the giant you have set your eyes on to defeat. The term for such an individual is a *Mentor*. The other vital reason you need a mentor is to help protect you from your "Kryptonite." Even Superman had a weakness. No matter how powerful and seemingly invincible he was, if he was exposed to Kryptonite for too long, it could have dire consequences. For each of us, we have our own "Kryptonite," called *Blind spots,* which can be equally devastating if not identified and guarded against. This is another key reason each of us *Need* a mentor in our life—to help us navigate around our weaknesses that we are often blinded to ourselves. Fortunately, with the support of a committed individual who cares about your long-term success, if you will pay attention to their advice, you can dodge the dangers that you might never see coming.

Now that you know what a mentor is, and I have hopefully properly convinced you that you need one, the question I am always asked is *"Where do you find one?"* Great question! I am so glad you asked! I would first recommend looking in your current *circle of connections*. In my life, I have enjoyed the privilege of several mentors speaking to me, although I often did not even recognize them as such at the time. As a few examples, here are a few of mine along the way. First, my Dad and my Mom were, but for completely different reasons. My Dad, Sam W. Hill, taught me a *strong* work ethic and how to be a Great Dad. He could not be outworked, and he was *Always* there for me . . . *Always*! My Mom, Myra J. Thornton Hill, was my example of *Dreaming* and *Faith*. She was my teacher in my faith in God and she proved the power of *dreaming* for more through her acts of faith. She was an entrepreneur who opened up in her living room and developed it into a multisite company. Their examples have served me very well in all my business dealings, and I question where I would be today had they not been such great parents. I also count my Grandparents as great mentors for my journey. My Pop, Jessie Hill, was a strong and tenacious man who would not quit regardless of the circumstances of his life. Even after having BOTH of his legs amputated at the knee, he tilled a massive garden each year, and he still taught himself how to drive a truck with foot pedals! You might see a little bit of where I get my tenacious "We can do this" spirit! My Grandaddy, LeRoy Thornton, was a pastor throughout my life. He often took me along with him as he would go and care for people. He taught me how to preach, how to speak to a crowd, how to pastor individuals, and how to dress like a Gentleman. I would like to think I'm a lot like them both. My Memaw, Maxine Thornton, taught me everything I know about prayer. She taught me that everything you do does not matter until you pray about it. As I look back across my life, it is every time that I have strayed from praying that I have been at my weakest. I am so eternally grateful for such an amazing woman of faith to mentor me in prayer by her living daily example. And for me, there have been *Many* great individuals who I would now call mentors. My first boss, Barry Reed; my Youth Pastor, David Akridge; my Uncle and Pastor of many years, Kevin Thornton/KT; my college professor, Mark Harris (who kept me from being kicked out of college . . . I am VERY grateful for that guy!); an Oklahoma leader and a part of my personal Board of Life, Wes Lane; and John Howry, who is an older friend who has expanded my *Exposure* to social issues, politics, business, etc., in many ways. The funniest part, is as I sit here typing this, *I am realizing how many Amazing people it has taken on my journey for me to have just this honor of writing this book for you!* And had I not taken the time to pursue just one of them, how differently my path might have turned. Yet the above list does not even include all the *Multitude* of *Teachers* and *Authors* who heavily influenced me through their work or books they wrote! I am the recipient of a vast education I received by modeling the examples each of them displayed. I am so truly *Grateful* for all my mentors along the way, and that is why *I implore you to pursue mentors for your life.*

For you, this might be a parent, a family member, a teacher, a coach, a business owner, a pastor, and often you can find them at your church. In my experience, these potential mentors seem like "everyday people" who do everyday things, but you will recognize that they do things in an *Excellent* way. Such individuals are also leaders who love to share their experiences and who most importantly care about your success in life. If you already know someone like that, it's time to ask them if they have some time to answer a few questions that would help you reach your goals. It's really that simple to start when you already know them. So, go for it!

But what if you feel as though no one in your life currently is committed to mentor you toward achieving your dreams? Although I would question such a reality because most of us have at least someone, but if you do not, then it's time to *Add* some new individuals into your life. So, ask yourself, *"If my dream is to become a _____, then who should I be sitting with? Who should I ask to Mentor me?"* Are you missing opportunities you should be seizing because you do not have the right relationships? Once you've answered those questions, it's time for you to respond! Seek out others who desire to help you grow and take them to lunch. Pursue relationships with individuals who will benefit you and whom you also can help grow by caring about them. If you make them a priority and add benefit to their lives also, you will find a truly successful relationship that will grow and last for years to come.

The true key to this rule is in surrounding yourself with people who care about you but who think outside the box and see life, business, achievement and the "impossible" differently. Each of us need someone that perceives what is possible or impossible differently than we have. Such exposure will ALWAYS result in growth. *If you do not have such individuals in your life, you will always have the same perspective until you change your proximity to those who have envisioned more for themselves and for you.* Although if you are determined, you will likely reach the success you are pursuing without a mentor, but I dare say that it will likely take you twice as long . . . So be smart and seek out wise voices in life. Find a *Mentor.*

#29

SAVE.
TODAY'S RESOURCE IS SEED
FOR TOMORROW'S SUCCESS.

A generation ago, there was a way to "retire comfortably," which was produced by people putting back a portion of their income or revenues for the future or by developing a company, which would provide passive income throughout their lives plus leave an inheritance for their children. The vast majority now believe that the Government will subsidize their golden years. This is a Myth. It is your responsibility to prepare for your future, not anyone else's. Create money-generating opportunities such as passive income, put back a portion of your monthly income into savings, or just stuff money into a 401k up to the limit! Cut back. Tighten the belt. Sell unnecessary items to purchase other items to sell for a profit. Find ways through your interest to provide for other people's needs or wants. In short, create your own *savings* plan and stick with it! It just might be the resource you need to make your future successes a reality.

#30

BUILD A LIFE STATEMENT.

Who are you and who do you want to be? Notice I did not ask "what do you want to be?" because these two things of *who* and *what* are very different. Although *who* you want to be can effect and even help decide *what*, but *what* should NEVER decide *who*. So, *what's* the difference? "What" is *something you do*, while "who" is *something you are*. "What" is a vocation while "who" is an *identity*. "What" can be *a changing action* while "who" is *a constant growing reflection of your character*. "Why is this important?" you may ask. Because *if* who *you are is wrapped up in* what *you are, then if* what *you are changes, then you will be confused about* who *you are*. Through the eye of media, we see many examples of this conflict of identity in celebrities and pro athletes. At one moment, they are award winning, *paparazzi* following *mega stars* with loads of *fame* and finance with groupies and fans that follow. However, as seasons change, so does their popularity. Individuals who the masses once wood stand in line for hours to just catch a glimpse now no longer care if they're standing next to them in Starbucks. A dear friend who felt this transition said it to me like this, "When you're in, you're in, but when you're out, you're out." Although not all of us will be celebrities, we all will face this change of seasons in one fashion or another. For some, it's transitioning from being the super popular all-state high school athlete to graduating and going into the workforce where no one cares about your record or accomplishments on the field. For many, it's in the transition from being successful with a career to changing companies unexpectedly because of layoffs. And in all these, we cannot change the what that is often out of our control.

This is why it is so very important that *who you* are is not defined by *what* you do. That is why a life statement is so important. As seasons and careers change, if you know who you are (that is your identity), then even though your circumstances will be different, you will never get lost in the confusion of the change.

All right, now that I have you convinced of the need, so *what is a life statement* and *how do you build one*? I'm glad you asked. First off, I used the word *build* in developing your life statement because I like to think of it as a rough draft that will need to be changed and adjusted overtime as you grow to mature in your identity. For example, my life statement at eighteen would have been different from the one I live my life by now. The wording I would have used and even some of the things I would have thought more important then would not even make the list now. And that is okay.

In life, as our seasons change, what we view as a priority also often change. That is why I believe first you must start your statement with your core values. Values are those deep beliefs that truly *define who you are* as an individual. It is it is rare for one's values to change, and therefore, they are the best place to begin.

As an example, here is my personal *Life Statement*, "I was born at this time in *History* to *Live* for the *Glory* of God, the *Growth* of His *Kingdom*, and the *Benefit* of His *People*, knowing that I have been positioned at this time and place to *Know* God in an intimate daily walk and *Make Him Known* to my *Family* and to the *World* that is within my *Radius*."

In the statement, you can see a snapshot of my core values and the beliefs that make me who I am. Notice, although I love being an entrepreneur and public speaker, I did not mention those career opportunities in my statement. After all, those are the *what*, not the *who*. Although mine was based in my faith in my Creator, yours might look totally different, and that is all right also. Start with what you know and believe be willing to adapt your statement to your ever growing maturity and knowledge, and never ever get "who you are" mixed with "what you do." If you will pursue these steps to building a *Life Statement*, I believe you will avoid the pitfalls of society and life that will try to define you by the what rather than the who. I believe by doing this, you will achieve much greater things through your life. Just a thought . . .

#31

LEARN FROM YOUR HISTORY OR BE FORCED TO REPEAT IT. IGNORANCE IS NO EXCUSE.

Simply put, *grow* wiser from your mistakes and the mistakes of others. We all make mistakes. However, rather than choosing to be different, how often do we repeat the same ones over and over and over? Yet using good judgment helps us learn from our previous actions. Inadequate knowledge causes us to continue on a faulty path. And while often it just seems easier to follow the same old path because we find it comfortable there, what if we choose to think and act differently? What opportunities could it open for our lives? What we do know, however, is that if we continue to do the same mistakes that we have watched in the lives of those before us and continue to repeat the faults of our own past, we will continue to get the same results. While going forward stretches us to change, when we finally change, we can look back and realize we were stuck in the mundane, often painful, rut of history . . . and no one really wants to live in their past.

So, let's choose to not continue repeating the same aching and often humiliating errors of yesterday. Let's learn from those monstrous mistakes that have grieved us for too long, because the truth remains that if we fail to change we will fail to succeed. Therefore, tell your yesterday's good-bye and reach out for a new tomorrow!

#32

DON'T BUY UNTIL YOU SLEEP ON IT.

We've all heard it . . . "This offer ends today. I can only 'guarantee' this price until you walk out the door." I call this the pressure to buy game. These phrases and many others like them are sales tactics used to convince people to purchase before they properly think it through. The idea is to create a "high pressure" situation that makes you think that something you "want" will be unreachable if you do not buy it at this exact moment. This type of commerce feeds on the dramatic and our desire for instant gratification—both which can be detrimental to our future. It has been a destructive force for many individuals and *families* by which they chain themselves to high-interest long-term loans, which are next to impossible to ever pay off, sacrificing a brighter future for a shimmering moment. Fortunately, however, you are *Different*! You have decided you want more from your life and for your future family! So here is how you accomplish that goal.

First, determine that before you ever walk in to make a major life-altering decision before you sign on the line, you are going to leave and sleep on it. That is 90 percent of the battle! Making that decision before you're ever in the situation sets the boundaries and gives you freedom to find clarity before making a long-term agreement. It empowers you with a sensibility that most buyers do not have and that also gives you negotiating power.

Secondly, be bold. Let the salesman or potential employer know that before you sign on the line or accept the job offer, you need to take the proper time to process this commitment. This can create a much more comfortable environment and decreases the feelings that can come from unmet expectations (which is one of the top causes of conflict!).

On to the third, which is *be* willing to let it go. I understand that this is the most difficult part of all. You see it. You want it! And now, you have this person telling you can have it. So why am I trying to block you? I'm not, you are . . . Because you are different! You desire to be successful and the only way to achieve that is to be different than the norm. In order to truly become successful and make great deals, you must be willing to walk away. You must accept, today just might not be the day. This particular car or house or anything . . . just might not be the right exact one. In fact, in truth, there is likely one much better just down the road, but you must wait for it . . . and that's not fun. However, that is the beginning of success! This is because *the man who can walk away has power in negotiating and in reasoning over the terms and conditions to which he is willing to commit himself.* Be that successful individual by being bold, be willing to walk away and always, always, always sleep before you buy.

#33

GIANTS.

It's been a while sense I faced a true *Giant*. I have faced battles and even *Wars* throughout the last few seasons, but it's been a time since I stared down a giant. It's been awhile since I considered standing up to an adversary who could defeat me in my own strength. Yesterday, such a *Giant* roared across the field. At first, I was excited yet apprehensive... Let's call it cautiously optimistic... for you see I have known since youth that I would face giants and stand before kings. However, when you see the size of the giant in person and see how small you are in comparison, it's very easy to become frightened. Over the last twenty-four hours, I have struggled with multiple emotions, including just heading back home! But if I am honest, isn't that what most people do? Because of apprehension or anxiety, they just choose to not go onto the field of battle? It's safer that way. Rather than risking a loss to a giant, it's easier to just return home. No one will know . . . but you. You, in your old age, when youthful ambition and middle age tenacity have passed, YOU will know. You will remember that once upon a time, when your hair wasn't as gray, that *you* had the opportunity to stand up to a giant . . . and you did nothing. This may be private knowledge only to you, that you coward when you could have conquered, but it will be a story you tell yourself as long as you breathe. *Although no one else may judge you, you will hold court of your choice with a plaintiff and defendant of one.* So, what shall we do concerning the *Giants* we face on this field?

Here are a few points that I think we need to remember.

1. I am constantly reminding myself that God did not make the giant any shorter nor easier for David to defeat. Rather David's God became bigger than the *giant*. How big is your belief in God? The answer to that question will determine much more than your size or that of the giant.

2. *Faith*. I've often told kids throughout the years that God will never allow you to live a life where faith is an option. Today, I am feeling the weight of those words and the reality of that truth. The Bible says that without "Faith," it is impossible to please God. The scripture even states that *Faith* is the substance of things hoped for and the evidence of things not seen. Let me simplify that. Faith is the foundation for everything that you believe can come to be (what you are dreaming of) and it is the substance to prove what you can't see yet with your eyes is actually there or coming . . . That's powerful. So, that means if God put it in my heart and I will *Choose* to believe, then ALL things are possible . . . even defeating the giants that oppose that dream that God gave me.

3. Faith without action isn't enough. I knew I was gifted to be an entrepreneur, but I had to step out in faith, make some sacrifices and bust some concrete before it ever happened. If you believe you are supposed to play college or professional sports, you must work out and practice to develop your body before you will ever see the scholarship or contract. If you want to be a doctor, lawyer, teacher, or anything specific, you must commit to that goal, lay aside everything that could hold you back and study to acquire the prize. If you believe it, then you must make the tough choices to go for it.

4. Be careful who's advice you take when consider facing giants. this is the time in your life to seek counsel of those who have defeated giants themselves, not just spectated from a distant safety. It's difficult for those who are not

called to kill giants to guide those who are called. After all, if they were called to conquer your giants, then they would have already.

5. The giants you fight today will provide the swords for the battles you face tomorrow. Therein, should you not face or defeat the giant today, you will not be equipped to win the fights in your future. Pray and Persevere today because today's wins (and losses) prepare you for you for the journey ahead . . . which just might include even taller giants and an insane spear-throwing King.

At the end of the day, everyone at some point in their life has a dream, yet many will never pay the price to acquire it. Why you may ask? Because Giants are scary, and we are told that they will devour us in our own strength. Although this might be true, they are nothing more than big bullies waiting to fall to a person who is willing to believe and take the field of Faith. So, go ahead and take your field, face your giant for one day it just might be his sword that you use to win an even greater wars. Just a thought . . .

#34

DON'T JUST MAKE RESOLUTIONS, LIVE RESOLUTE.

"Whether you think you can or can't, you are right," (Henry Ford).

Resolutions are a funny thing. Each year at the end of December a few days after Christmas, people often begin to evaluate the issues or places in their lives that they are the least pleased with and, thereby, decide to "make a resolution" to change that habit or situation in the New Year. All too often, these resolutions do not last past the first few weeks after being declared. Why? If these individuals, who became aware of something in their life which they wanted to see changed, then why did they not stay committed to that goal? It's because their resolution was an idea based on information rather than resolute determination based in need.

In order for you to succeed, you must determine to succeed at the same level of commitment you have to the act of breathing. You must desire the success of your goal with that same tenacity.

There's a story of two kids, from the same neighborhood, with the same family structure, race and socio-economic struggles who attend the same school. Both young men were very similar in all the ways that count except one. Years later, once they had grown up, one became Founder and CEO of a Fortune 500 company while the other bounced from job to job and struggled from paycheck to paycheck. What is the one consistent factor that I've seen *stand out* above all the rest? Determination.

Although both young men had massive hurdles to cross to reach their dreams, one determined to be resolute in reaching his goals while the other allowed the circumstances of his life to determine his potential. Oftentimes one chooses to allow negative influences to affect the direction he or she takes. You must choose to be strong and determined to be your best. These negative influences can only be overcome by the choices you make . . . by living resolute. Just a thought . . .

#35

IF YOU WANT TO DO GREAT BIG THINGS, DO SMALL THINGS GREAT.

Everybody I sit with wants to do *Big Things*! Big, BIG, BIG Things! *Monumental, Huge, Massive, Venti, BIG Things!* I yet to meet with any-one who says, "You know, Brian, I really want to do small things!" Just has not happened at the printing of this book. I get it. I totally understand why. I desire to do BIG, BIG, BIG things! I want to make a lasting mark in my radius and for the WORLD to have a reason to know I was here! I think *Big*. I dream *Big*. I want *Big*. I want to do *Big* things.

But too often, we get our eyes on the wrong things and we fail to realize that to accomplish *Big* things we must first do Small things. You see, nothing ever begins Big. It just does not work that way. It must start tiny and develop into maturity over time . . . and that is all right. In fact, if it did not start small and gradually grow into its capacity, it could not sustain its potential size. Imagine if a skyscraper was constructed to its maximum height before the foundation was even laid. It would crumble before they even reached its prospective pinnacle. So why do we expect to reach the top before we have pro-duced a proper base to construct upon? Simply put, *to get big, you must first focus on the small!*

The key is to *Focus on the details.* It is the small things done well that make the difference in the long term. It is the attention we give to the seemingly insignificant everyday mundane stuff that positions us and our dreams to develop into a reflection of our goals . . . and such things cannot be rushed. So often we are tempted to take short-cuts along life's path. There are no microwave solutions for long-term success and the trustworthy way to achieve gigantic opportunities is to have laser focus on compact details with excellence. It will likely be the consistent excellent work on the items that others overlook that will likely produce your successes. Dr. Martin Luther King Jr. once said, "If a man is called to be a street sweeper, he should sweep streets even as Michelangelo painted or Beethoven composed music or Shakespeare wrote poetry. He should sweep streets so well that all the hosts of heaven and earth will pause to say, 'Here lived a great street sweeper who did his job well.'" What if you committed to the tedious details of your ambitions in such a way as for the "hosts of heaven and earth" to pause and notice? Doesn't that sound like a recipe for success? With a plan like that, don't you think you can build an "Empire"? Sounds good, but it starts with focusing today on writing that essay that's due next week. It begins with showing up five minutes early for work and staying five minutes later than every-one else. So rather than rushing through an assigned detail, consider what the end result will look like and give it the needed finishing touch of excellence. Rather big or small, choose to do things to the best of your ability and the product will speak for you in the long game. Always remember that small things done well will produce big results. After all, *success* will happen because you live committed day by day to generate solid results on the menial task that produce extraordinary results over time. So, do small things with big effort. You will eventually reap *Big* results. Just a thought . . .

#36

WHEN THE WOLVES ARE AT THE DOOR, DON'T MAKE DINNER FOR THEM.

Too often when public figures get attacked by the media, they *react*, making an even larger spectacle of themselves. They say something inappropriate or act out, giving their critics even more ammo for their attack. It all too often becomes a *he said, she said* deal that gets uglier with each response. We witness this behavior in every area of our lives and careers also. In sports, the opposition taunts you to get you angry, resulting in you "dropping the ball." In business, your competitors or coworkers position themselves for you to slip when questioned. And ladies, on social media a "friend" of yours calls you a name in response to a post you made about a puppy you thought was "cute" and she said you were calling her names because *cute* doesn't actually mean "cute," and you were saying all of this because you are trying to "steal her boyfriend." And as ridiculous as all of this sounds, it has become *Normal* in our American society. Yet none of this useless *Drama* should be part of our lives.

The only way to stop it is to choose to not participate in it. Yes, I understand, it is VERY difficult but necessary if we desire to live a life of peace. So how are we going to accomplish that? The important lesson to learn from these examples is to keep a *Cool* head. In the real *World*, you cannot *beat them up* for *making fun of your Mama!* Instead, you focus hard and *prove their words to be false. Stay Calm* and do not feed their words. The Chinese have a proverb that speaks with wisdom gleaned over centuries. It simply says, "*He who treads softly goes far.*" So, do not make yourself a buffet for the wolves. Let them find a meal at the door of someone who likes to live in drama. Choose to not play along. Just a thought . . .

#37

GO TOGETHER. GROW TOGETHER.

I love meeting with entrepreneurial *minds*. Possibilities expand in my life every time I sit with innovative souls. Too often, we view others as competition or we see connections as mere opportunities for our own benefit. But what if we viewed every contact from a "You grow, then I grow" viewpoint? Rather than making it all about me and what I can get from the relationship, what if I looked for ways to increase and create *Value* for them? In a "get mine first" world, this just seems strange, right? But I have found that every time I give of my time by sharing thoughts, suggestions or just listening for the benefit of another, I always receive. This type of partnership is not born in contracts or positions but rather in a commitment and loyalty to each other's success. Such a relationship breeds an environment of dual achievement! You literally develop a vehicle for you and your associates to thrive because of your proximity to one another. This type of connection becomes a living example of a "win-win" alliance!

Still critical? I understand. What I am suggesting in Not "normal." But I must ask, "Are you growing? Are you adding *Value* into someone else's life? Is the way you have previously viewed others (such as siblings, team-mates, coaches, professors, bosses, and even *parents* . . .) resulted in you achieving your vision of success?" If so, congratulations! Although you are possibly in denial, feel free to move on to the next chapter. However, if you are like most others, myself included, then there are a lot of opportunities you are currently missing out on. But that can also be exciting! That means that *today*, you can begin to look for those moments to encourage those in your life and be part of them reaching their pinnacle. That might commence with saying an encouraging word or giving a compliment or simply writing a Thank You note to express how something they did helped or inspired you. *We never truly know the impact that a simple act of kindness or appreciation will have on the life of another. It just might become the spark to their blaze.* After all, if we *Go Together*, we will no doubt *Grow Together*.

#38

THE VILEST VILLAIN OF ACHIEVEMENT IS ENTITLEMENT.

Entitlement. It steals possibilities and leaves only frustrations. It offers handout trinkets as a cheap substitute to earned accomplishments and innovation. It robs our society of fresh and witty creations. It is a jailer who shackles freedom in chains of dependence. How many young lives has it crushed in poverty? Entitlement truly is a damnable mind-set. It says that you owe me something that I have done nothing to earn. It is a jail of our own building with the cruelest of wardens who will keep us confined for a life sentence if we allow.

Once we accept that we are owed nothing in this life, we are Free to pursue a limitless sky of opportunities. You must work hard, make no excuses and commit to the cause. If you do, you just might reach your goals, but even if you do not, at least you will not get buried by a mediocre, entitled existence. Fight for your family's future. Choose to succeed, not to just survive.

#39

SEND HANDWRITTEN "THANK YOU" NOTES.

To most, it seems like an archaic thought to hand write a letter or card in this time of instant e-mails and text from our phones. Today if I want to share my feelings of appreciation, I can post it to social media, often before I can properly process my thoughts into words. If I want to say "Thanks," I can type it in two seconds and message in the next second. Quick. Clean. Efficient. But consider the value of receiving such a text or e-mail . . . How many quick correspondence have you received this week, today or even this hour? Think back to your last birthday. How many "friends" posted a birthday message to your wall and who were the people that sent those? Now, how many actual birthday cards did you receive and from whom?? I really can't name five of the social media wishes, yet I can name all three individuals who sent me actual cards. There simply is something more powerful about a tangible touchable note that I can hold in my hand.

Take that same example and apply it to your next important interview, dinner, or meeting. Rather than e-mailing your appreciation for the opportunity to interview with the college admissions or company hiring manager, what if you also handwrote a Thank You note? Among the other applicants who just sent e-mails, would you stand out? After meeting with a potential client, what if you followed up with every one of them with a personalized hand-scripted note of thanks? Do you think it would make a difference on the bottom line for your company sales?

I learned this immensely effective point for success from a *very* affluent and wise entrepreneur investment banker who I shall refer to as AW. While sitting in his office for a few valuable minutes, AW asked me if I ever sent out Thank You notes, to which I ashamedly said no. He began to tell me that writing such notes is a normal part of his day and a key to much of his success with long-term clients. AW shared that each evening, after a long day at the office and at meetings with clients, as he sat relaxing, he would handwrite Thank You cards to every individual he met with that day. He would then mail them out the following day, knowing that individual would receive them within seventy-two hours of their initial meeting. Such a practice has accomplished multiple traceable results, but the two that I will share are, first it serves as a follow-up reminder of the details of their discussion and secondly, it produces a very positive view of AW as a gentleman who cares enough about his clients and associates to take the time to express appreciation. Thus, both come back to *it makes them feel important* . . . and don't we ALL want to feel important to those we do life with? Doesn't the hiring manager or the college admissions director or your boss or your Mom want to feel like you noticed them? For that matter, doesn't *everybody*? The simple answer is *Yes*. So, take the time to hand write a Thank You note every time you meet with someone and see what the long-term results will be. Feel free to drop a thank you card in the mail to my office *when* you see it working for you!

#40

CHOOSE WISELY. YOUR DECISIONS TODAY WILL DETERMINE YOUR TOMORROWS.

When I was a kid, my Pop (my Dad's Dad) planted a garden every spring. I would help him plant the seeds in beautifully straight rows. Months later, I would help him deweed the plants and eventually assist Pop in harvesting the vegetables and fruits. That season in my young life taught me the *Principles of Sowing and Reaping*. Jesus says in the Bible that "as a man soweth so shall he reapeth." I have never placed a jalapeno pepper seed in the ground and harvested a roma tomato as its produce, nor have I picked a poblano pepper from a squash vine. What you plant you WILL pick. This is a consistent principle throughout our world.

As such, the decisions you plant in your life today will determine the harvest you reap in your life for your tomorrows. If you choose to accept compromise of your values such as cheating, stealing, and sleeping around, then you will reap the consequences of broken trust, possible incarceration, and broken relationships. If you live beyond your means, impulse-shop, and purchase on credit, you will dig a pit of debt that can consume your financial future. Buy a $50 sweater today on sale for $20, but use a credit card with 22 to 28 percent interest and end up paying $120 for it by the time you pay it off with compound interest . . . Not very smart, right?

On the other side of that card, choosing to go to a smaller college which offers the same degree as the large university, but offers more scholarships, allowing you to not take out $50,000 plus in loans. Rather than buying a new car with your first "real job," you instead save up and purchase a used car that you can pay cash for, thus allowing you to continue saving rather than buying debt and working to pay a car payment (plus insurance and tag which is higher for a new car). Rather than jumping into a relationship, take your time to get to know the individual, ask them important questions, meet their friends, and see how they take care of their stuff (clothes, car, etc.). Consider this, you go out with someone for a couple of dates, find them *extremely* attractive, put yourself in a compromised situation and you both end up with a child together nine months later. Where will you both spend the holidays? Where will you and the child live? If you are going off to college, will you still be able to go? You have a child you are responsible for now. What if you realize in the stress of being up late at night with a crying baby, bills and lost opportunities, that you don't even "like" this person you share a child with? This one night decision, created by attraction and lust, will bind you together, in one form of relationship or another, for the rest of your lives and affect EVERY decision that follows . . . Complicated, right? Every decision of your life will ultimately have positive or negative consequences, some for the rest of your life. *Choose Wisely.*

#41

LOOSE LIPS SINK SHIPS.

A man of quiet resolve is an asset to a friend and a danger to all who call him adversary.

Too often, we speak *Everything* we are thinking to *Everyone* we encounter and then we wonder why people share our personal information *Everywhere* they go. When I was very young, my Mom quoted a scripture from Proverbs 17:28, which says, "*Even a fool is thought wise when he shuts his lips.*" I have carried that bit of wisdom throughout life. Although I have not lived by this principle to the extent I wish I had, it has kept me from many pointless arguments that I would have engaged in otherwise. At its core, this principle is about fighting our need as a society to always have something to say to make us look better to others. We *all* want to be important in the eyes of those we look up to, so often we share any secrets (a.k.a. gossip) about others, and sometimes ourselves, in an attempt to gain the attention of that Very Important Person. This is typically because we want this VIP to want to spend more time with us *learning from all the amazing information that we have that they need* . . . Unfortunately, this desire is birthed from a place of insecurity and a lack of self-confidence . . . and in truth, Most of us have shared something we should not have for this reason.

It's tough. I get it. However, we must choose, as part of our character to be a safe and trusted place for the information that would hurt those who trust us. If your friend has *eleven* toes and he is embarrassed by it, do not share it with the guys in the locker room. Should you find out that your best friend pees her pants every time she laughs to hard (true story), as much fun as it would be to make a joke about it, it is not your place to tell. Even if you find out that the scourge of your life who has always been mean to you, that his parents are getting divorced for some horrible reason, you must choose to live with integrity and not blast it out. I understand these things might seem silly and somewhat insignificant, but eventually a friend will need someone that they can trust with something big and in that moment, you just might be the listener they need to help them through their dark hour of life. But such moments are built on a lifetime of trust. So be authentic. Be *real* and do *not* tell every detail you hear to everyone you know. The day will likely come when you will be glad you did.

*   *   *

Let me be clear, all the above items refer to items of a personal embarrassing nature. However, if you become aware of someone (friend or not) who is considering hurting themselves or others, YOU have a responsibility to immediately speak with a trusted adult or authority. If YOU are hurting from being hurt by someone else or you are considering hurting yourself, PLEASE share your pain with a trusted adult who cares. A Teacher, Professor, Coach, Pastor, or Counselor . . . Somebody. Because YOU Matter and You will make a difference. This is one of the highest forms of Integrity and a necessity for your friend and anyone else whom their actions could harm. This is the time that talking could Save a Life!

#42

EVEN WHEN YOU ARE LOSING THE GAME. DON'T QUIT.

My son Josiah plays baseball, so many of our weekends have been shared at the ballfields watching countless games. His very first season, his team went undefeated. It was quite an accomplishment for a group of five-year-olds. However, the next season, a team from out of area moved into the league. The evening they took the field to compete against this new team, we learned they had won the State Championship in the division the previous year. I saw something different in my son's team that night. Before the first ball was even hit, they had already lost. Although his team had won the league the previous year, they were so afraid that they could not beat the "State Champs" that they did not even give their best. They did not even *Try*. Now, in truth, that little team was "good." Real good. My son's team might have lost even if they had given their best, but the greatest loss that evening was they did not play to win. More than losing to a team, they lost to *Fear*.

Many times, if we perceive that we cannot win, that the odds are against us or we do not match up; we just do not even make an attempt. If we are honest, this is a reaction to *Fear*. If we try and do not succeed, what will our family or our friends or strangers on social media think of us? If we try and fail, does that make us a failure? And so, many do not even make attempt for fear of losing should they try. What they fail to see in this lack of trying is that the greater loss they concede to is in failing to try.

This unseen fear is one of the worst kinds. This type of fear, though silent and hidden, is vicious, for it kills the very seed of success before it can be planted. Countless great companies, inventions, innovations and social successes have been devoured within the minds of those who coward to this dark enemy. Innumerable athletes and scholars did not accept the challenges before them of going to college (and staying in) due to the very thought of not being able to make it. Questions of "what if" and "what then" and "what will they say should I fail?" cripple them in mediocrity.

But you are different. Although you will face giants and adversaries too great to conquer, you will not quit.

Regardless of their record or who is in their corner, you will still take the field with confidence. Even though it seems foolish because they outnumber you ten to one or they have all the money in the world, you will still commit to win. For you are a David. Although the entire army of Israel had shrunk in intimidation to the giant, young teenage David believed he could (and should) take down the enemy. Even though the odds were insurmountable against him, he chose to step onto the field. Not only did he defeat Goliath that day, but he eventually became king as a result of his boldness. When everyone else had hidden, David choose to *not quit*.

The truth is you may not "win." You might lose the game, the election, the deal or whatever it is, but it is far better to try and not succeed than to never try. President Theodore Roosevelt once wrote, "Far better it is to dare mighty things, to win glorious triumphs, even though checkered by failure, then to take rank with those poor spirits who neither enjoy much nor suffer much, because they live in the gray twilight that knows not victory nor defeat." At the end of the contest, even if the outcome is not what you had hoped for, you might just find out that a much greater giant fell before you than the opponent on the other team and that wicked mammoth is called *fear of the unknown*. So, don't quit.

One last thought I once heard a preacher say, "Don't cry to quit. Cry to keep going. You're already in pain," so *Make* it count and *Don't Quit*. Because *You've Planted* seed, You're Due a Harvest IF you just don't *Quit*. Let's continue to move forward Ladies and Gents because *Quitting is not an option*.

#43

WORDS PRODUCE PERCEPTION.

Words Matter. Something as simple as using the word *Yes* or *Yea* can make a huge difference when meeting a potential employer or college recruiter for the first time. Each word produces an idea of the type of person I am and the level of education I have earned. When my name is called, responding with "Yes?" versus "What?" leaves individuals with a perception of my background, and thus, my future. Words have impact. In this generation, especially, we hear individuals saying, "Don't judge me," yet we deny the reality that we each make judgments of every individual we meet based on our initial perception. If the cashier greets you warmly with a bright smile and a courteous "Hello," your entire perception of that store and shopping experience can instantly be transformed into a positive encounter, thus increasing the probability that you will return to shop there again. However, in the exact same store with an employee who makes no eye contact and says, "Yea, what do you need?" the experience and thus the result will be much different. Your judgments about the store would be based on the *positive* or *negative* feelings you had to the words and actions of the employee, subconsciously believing that "the store" did or did not care about you as a customer. Make no mistake, your view as a shopper will not only effect the business, but rather it will equally impact the employee eventually (lost sales cause lost profits which results in lost payroll for the employee).

As I mentioned previously in chapter 16, I was hired into a manager position of a large company because I was the only individual to "ever" wear a tie for the interview at that store; however, my use of language also played a key part in that opportunity and the resulting opportunities that subsequently have followed. By simply using words like *yes*, *ma'am*, and *sir*, I expressed a level of respect and maturity that an employer desired to be represented in their company. Nothing complicated, just simple classic manners, yet uncommon in our current society. This lack of common courtesy, however, can serve as a benefit for you *if you* simply choose to represent yourself well by using the most simplistic of proper terms . . . y merely saying *yes*. After all, *words* matter!

#44

IT'S NOT JUST WHO YOU KNOW, BUT HOW YOU TREAT WHO YOU KNOW.

A friend of mine named John Howry shared this principal with me and I have valued it ever since. I had always been told that "it's not what you know, but who you know"; however, this simple yet poignant twist made a significant difference in my understanding of this valuable principle.

Consider this: what if the successful achievement of your dream in life was affected either positively or negatively by each and every relationship you have or will develop throughout your life? *What if the people in your life actually hold the key to the door of your life goals?* Do you find that thought concerning? You should because how you treat people today will affect your future, whether positively or negatively. *When you begin to view each and every person that comes into your life as the individual who could make your life dream possible, you will absolutely treat everyone with the respect that they deserve.* So be thankful for who you know and remember to treat them with the utmost respect . . . They just might hold the keys to your future.

#45

SWING DEEP

"Don't let the fear of striking out keep you from playing the game" (Babe Ruth).

This is the quote I shared with my son Josiah recently. I was noticing that he was struggling to hit anything in a game. In practice, he would hit three out of four, but as soon as he stepped up to the plate, it was nothing. During our talk, I realized that He was so afraid of getting out that he was locking up mentally and could not hit the ball, thus fulfilling his fear.

How often do we as adults live our lives in the same way? Because of our fear of failure due to the unknown, we back off any opportunity and accept defeat before the final play. But we were never meant to live our lives in such a fashion. As Christians, our very foundation is built upon the miraculous. We are the people who are called to the seemingly impossible. The very core of all that we believe in calls us to walk our journey on the tumultuous waters by His design. And yet, while, we know this to be true—living out such seems irrational to the common man . . . but you were *Never* meant to be *Common*! You are designed as a complex work of art in a life-long process of being molded, crafted for a specific purpose which only you can fulfill. But you will *only* achieve that success if you try.

For Josiah, it was a matter of him choosing *not to fear* the strike out. For you, what is it you are not trying for fear of failure?

I'm proud to say that because Josiah changed his mind-set on striking out; he has made at least 1 great hit per game since his decision, resulting in several runs for his team (three hits in a game last week!). So, let's learn from the examples before us! Let's swing deep for our dreams and go for it! Holding nothing back, let's run our race with everything that's in us and play the game! Just a thought . . .

#46

WALK BY FAITH, NOT BY SIGHT.

Faith. Trust. If we are honest, these are difficult concepts for most of us to live out. If we cannot see it, how can we believe it? Right? Yet when I got up this morning, I did not fear that I would float off into space. Although I cannot see *gravity* holding me safely to Earth, I simply "knew" that I would not float away. That sense of "knowing" is merely *Faith* in action. Faith is simply trusting that although I cannot know the answer at this moment, I still can know the One who holds the answer I seek. I know, I know . . . The process is hard. It's trying. It can wear you down. I'm sure David, (1 Samuel 22) before he became King, felt much the same while hiding in a cave. But he had to walk by faith and reflect to younger days as a boy when he conquered a lion, a bear and a giant . . . All of which he defeated through *Faith* with nothing more than a rock and a slingshot in his hand. In the same way, remind yourself today of the last victory that you had! Maybe it was passing a test or being accepted into a specific *university* or getting a job; but reflect on that Win. Because the very same Creator that brought you through that is the same God who is faithful to bring you through this. Although you do not see the answer or the solution right now, your God, your Creator is at work in the background, producing a magnificent story from the pieces of your life. Just keep walking it out until you see it! Just a thought . . .

#47

What's in your Hands?

I have counseled a lot of ambitious individuals who desire to be entrepreneurs over the last several years and one trend I have continually noticed is most have a long-term dream, but few have a plan on how to get to it. In fact, most startups that I have seen fail were destroyed by individuals reaching for the long-term dream today rather than building it step by step overtime. Too often, with a large overhead as a result of a misguided starting loan, many fledgling companies are smothered by high overhead with little beginning cash flow resulting in *financial* destruction before they really had an opportunity for proof of concept. So then, if an individual has a dream and wants to start a company, how should they attempt to begin you ask? In my opinion, you start with what you have and simply ask "What's in my Hands?"

In the Old Testament of the Bible, there is a story of a man named Moses. While out in the field one day in hiding, Moses saw a burning bush. As he went to see the bush, he realized that although it was on fire, it was not being consumed. Suddenly, Moses began to hear a voice coming from the bush, which called his name. As the shepherd questioned the identity of the voice, he learned the voice of God was giving him a life mission. The Creator tells Moses that he had heard the prayers and cries of his people who were slaves in Egypt and desired to free them to a land of promise. Moses, likely being shocked by all of this, asked the Lord, "Who shall I tell them sent me?" To which God said, "Tell them I am." At this point, one would think that the burning bush and the audible voice of God might be enough, but like us, it was not enough for Moses either, so he asked for a sign. At this point of the conversation, God asked a question that still confounds human wisdom . . . "What's in your hands?" Simple answer was a shepherd staff. A long stick that he used to guide and protect helpless simple sheep, however in the hands of a man on a mission sent by God, it became a tool of deliverance. As you are reading this simple collection of thoughts today, I cannot help but ask ...and wonder "What's in your hands?" For Moses, it was a stick. For me, it was a seemingly insignificant company that my Mom had begun, which I initially wanted nothing to do with. However, just as Moses used that simple stick to deliver God's chosen people to the promised land, he used my Mom's small startup in my hands to begin a Preschool that would grow into a beautiful resource for education that would eventually provide the foundation for multiple other Companies and Ministries.

What's in your hands today might not look like much to you or to others, yet it just might be the tool that God uses to deliver your dream. Although it is small and simple and seemingly insignificant, do not discount what God can do with what you already have if you will merely trust him and allow him to. So once again I must ask, what's in your hand?

Just an Extra Thought . . .

Death of a Dream. Birth of a Vision.

We all have dreams as kids. We want to be a fireman, a doctor, an athlete, a teacher, or an astronaut. As adults, we are often the same. We dream of a promotion, a better job, a larger house, the perfect spouse, a dream car, exotic vacation, retirement or financial independence. Our dreams are as many as the sands of the seas. I once had a dream . . . the wife, the house, the car, the LIFE.

By some observations, I was successful. I had achieved marginal success for a twenty-something. I had purchased my first house, married a beautiful woman, bought a new BMW, and earned multiple promotions. At twenty-five, I really thought I had "achieved something." I did not realize at that moment in time that I was simply in training for the real journey. Although I had "success" at getting my "Dreams," my life was on a path to destruction and failure. I now realize that what you view as success is not a stamp of approval by God nor is it proof that you are in His will for your life. The truth is you must "seek God first" to fulfill His will for your life. In 3 John 2, the apostle writes, "Beloved, I wish above all things that thou mayest prosper and be in health, even as thy soul prospers."

Too often, we mistake *Dreams* for *Visions*, yet they are not the same. In my experience, I have found that people often have received marginal provision due to marginal obedience. In May of the following year, after six months of struggling with the direction God was guiding me, I left that good paying, stable job and stepped onto the treacherous road of being an entrepreneur. In the corporate job, with some success, I was living the dream; however, when I finally responded to God's call toward His path for my life, I started living out a Vision. You see, simply put, a dream is built from man's sight while a Vision is a glimpse of God's potential plan for your life. I realize now that my dreams had to die before His Vision could be conceived in me. I had to let go of what I wanted to begin the journey toward what I Need and therein lies the greatest of truths, that we must die to ourselves so that He can live through us. In this way, Vision is the same as the *Salvation* we receive in Jesus Christ; in that we must believe in what we cannot humanly see yet. Although such Faith is intimidating and often frightening, it is necessary because anything that you can already see physically does not truly require a Vision to create. (These passages of scripture are also great resources for your journey: Luke 12:31; John 3:8; Romans 9:24.)

Vision is no small thing. A multitude of books, speeches and sermons are about Vision, yet most individuals can not actually explain it. So here is my attempt. Vision is like a baby in the womb. It causes great rejoicing when first conceived. The conception brings fulfillment to a need for both the deliverer and the receiver. It is the same with God and the visionary. The visionary walks around life desiring fulfillment and God desires to release His plan into the visionary's life. When the visionary finally forsakes all others, and comes to God in desire, the need is met. After conception, the Vision is acknowledged, whereby the visionary *needs* to tell everyone. "Something new will be born!" Then comes the growth of things not seen and the wait as the Vision develops. And the visionary must wait . . . and wait . . . and wait . . . and wait. This period is very difficult and often brings great frustration. For the visionary, it does not sit well to wait; however, waiting is crucial. If one does not wait, *Development* will not be *Complete*. This is why so many Visions (companies, ministries, careers, etc.) die every day.

I have come to believe that a Vision does not die due to a lack of zeal, but rather due to a lack of nurturing and growth. Just as growth takes time, so does a Vision. It will never develop instantly but it will always be worth the wait if proper time is allowed. And just as the infant child that is growing within the mother's womb causes the mother to be changed also; so does the Vision change the visionary. This time of change will either cause the visionary to draw closer to

God or to push away. Time will either teach the visionary to be humble or it will set a root of bitterness. It will soften or make callous, but there *Will* be change during this time.

This is necessary at its core because *Vision* by the very definition is "a sight of the distant." I must admit that when I first read those words in the dictionary, they struck me fairly hard. Once I realized that even by its very nature a *Vision* requires a *Journey*, I became more prepared for what it would require to reach it. In order to arrive at one's Vision, he or she *must* travel to it. Too often our instinct is to run toward the goal with sudden zeal without accounting for the distance. However, this course is a marathon rather than a sprint. A marathon runner understands that in order to win, he must keep a steady pace for he must have the same zeal and determination at the end as he did in the beginning. For lack of understanding and inability to pace for the finish line, that is why many Visions die.

Quite often in business and in church, we produce speed runners. We encourage young individuals to "go after their dreams" and "be all they want to be," but we fail to educate them of the price they must pay to reach their desired destination. We take the zeal of a youthful student and plug them into a "take the world by storm" without guiding them with words of tempered experience and optimistic caution. Rather than training them up like a child (over time with discipline, nurture, education, etc.), we send babes onto battlefields. Yet as a society, we wonder why so many startups fail each year. For the visionary, time passes. Months. Years. Sometimes Decades. And the growth continues. Sometimes ever so slightly and slowly . . . and then . . . It's time! The right time, the appointed time comes! You're ready! The Vis*ion is Ready*! Here it comes! PAIN!

PAIN! What? Yes, Pain. Followed by Frustration, Confusion, ANGER! "God, why did you do this to me?" This is all His fault!

At this moment of birth, we know we cannot turn back although we would like to. We have come too far. The time is now and we must push through. We are committed! Yet going any further is difficult and to strenuous. With all this pressure, we want to just scream!

And then . . . peace, joy, hope . . . God has moved! It's here, the vision is really here! Finally, you can see the vision! Yes, it's small. It's not the strong adult warrior vision you had imagined, but it is the beginning infant vision which will grow. What you have so longed for is finally in front of you. For you, maybe it's the completion of a building designed long ago. Possibly it is the opening of the doors of a women's shelter or an orphanage. Maybe it's the birth of a child, which the doctors said could not be bore. It could be graduation day from the university, knowing you were the first in your family to earn a diploma. For me, it was on October 13 of 2003, after four and a half months of blood, sweat and tears; finally opening the doors of our first company with three employees and two clients . . . But I *Finally* saw the *Vision*!

Now, just because the Vision is born and visible, does not mean you are done or that you have arrived. To the contrary, now the work Really begins. Just as a child, you must guide, raise and protect it to be everything that God conceived in you and ordained it to be. Whether it is the first day of your new company or of training camp after making the team; now is the time to give all for you must develop the vision. It will cost you sleep, time and entertainment. It will *not* often be fun. However, it *will* be worth it! When you celebrate the first-year anniversary of opening the doors or when you walk onto that field for the first time to the cheers of the crowd or when you dedicate the first child from that stage or deliver that baby . . . It WILL be worth it. It will hurt. It will humble you. It will likely take a long time. But it WILL be worth it. So, let the dreams die. Allow the *Vision* to be conceived and grow.

So live Bold. Be Courageous. Go for it.

In the words of President Roosevelt, "It is not the critic who counts; not the man who points out how the strong man stumbles, or where the doer of deeds could have done them better. The credit belongs to the man who is actually in the arena, whose face is marred by dust and sweat and blood, who strives valiantly; who errs and comes short again and again; because there is not effort without error and shortcomings; but who does actually strive to do the deed; who knows the great enthusiasm, the great devotion, who spends himself in a worthy cause, who at the best knows in the end the triumph of high achievement and who at the worst, if he fails, at least he fails while daring greatly. So, that his place shall never be with those cold and timid souls who know neither victory nor defeat." So, live *Bold*. Be *Courageous*. Go for it! Just a thought . . .

Closing Thought

Daily, I am reminded of our cultures debauchery and my concern grows for what this Young Generation will face in their time. We as a country have reasoned that we are wise, that we are great and that we have no need for "a God" who requires us to live a moral life, much less a sinless one. But truth remains and no generation can stand in obstinacy to the principles which provided for their comfort without enduring a great loss. For this sickness, only one cure remains, *Repentance*. Only true heart believing Repentance can hold the hand of judgment and draw the tide of mercy from God. Should we not make this vital choice at this critical moment in our Nation's history, I fear that the Freedom for which many have perished to provide for us and defend for other nations, will vanish within a generation.

The Rev. Billy Graham was recently quoted in an interview as saying "Our children are growing up in a 'lawless and wicked age,' infused with the philosophy of the Devil, who says, 'Do as you please.'" Further, rearing children in this culture is difficult because "we have taken God out of our educational systems and thought we could get away with it, we have sown the wind, and we are now reaping the whirlwind. We have laughed at God, religion and the Bible."

My prayer today, for the sake of this Nation and this young generation, is that we as a people of Faith in the One True God and His Son, Jesus Christ, will humble ourselves (lest ye be humbled) and pray, turn from our wicked ways, acknowledge Him and ask The Almighty to direct our path as a Nation, under God, once again. May God forgive us, May God restore us to His principles that produce true *Freedom*, and May God bless these United States of America.

In the words of President Roosevelt, "It is not the critic who counts; not the man who points out how the strong man stumbles,

117

or where the doer of deeds could have done them better. The credit belongs to the man who is actually in the arena, whose face is marred by dust and sweat and blood, who strives valiantly; who errs and comes short again and again; because there is not effort without error and shortcomings; but who does actually strive to do the deed; who knows the great enthusiasm, the great devotion, who spends himself in a worthy cause, who at the best knows in the end the triumph of high achievement and who at the worst, if he fails, at least he fails while daring greatly. So, that his place shall never be with those cold and timid souls who know neither victory nor defeat." So, live Bold. Be Courageous. Go for it! Just a thought . . .

"Rejoice in the Lord always. I will say it again: Rejoice! Let your gentleness be evident to all. The Lord is near. Do not be anxious about anything, but in every situation, by prayer and petition, with thanksgiving, present your requests to God. And the peace of God, which transcends all understanding, will guard your hearts and your minds in Christ Jesus. Finally, brothers and sisters, whatever is true, whatever is noble, whatever is right, whatever is pure, whatever is lovely, whatever is admirable—if anything is excellent or praiseworthy—think about these things" (Phil. 4:4–8)

About the Author

Samuel Brian Hill founded his first company, Babes & Gents Preschool of Oklahoma, in 2003. Since that time, he and his family have diversified with the creation of multiple companies including Kairos Investments & Venture Partners in 2007 and Foundation Learning Centers of Texas in 2014. He has additionally served as the Director of IMPACT OKC Magazine since 2012, as the Director of YFC OKC WEST since 2010 and as a Pastor to a multitude of young generation students since 2003. Brian is passionate about business ventures, advising entrepreneurs, providing guidance for companies, public speaking, conservative politics and personally buying/selling JEEP Wranglers. He is also a graduate of Southwestern Christian University in Bethany, OK.

Brian married his college sweetheart, Melissa, in 2001 and they have two beautiful children, Eleanor Grace & Samuel Josiah. He and Melissa partner in multiple companies together and love to travel with their children. Their family loves doing adventures, time at the Beach, Baseball games, road trips and horse riding. Although Brian was born in Trenton, Tennessee and Melissa in San Antonio, Texas; they have been residences of the Greater Oklahoma City area since 1998.

CPSIA information can be obtained
at www.ICGtesting.com
Printed in the USA
LVOW12s1123160817
545127LV00009BA/24/P